Ainsley Harriott's Barbecue Bible

BBC Books

Published by BBC Books, BBC Worldwide Ltd,
80 Wood Lane, London W12 0TT

First published 1997
Reprinted 1997 (three times), 1998 (three times)
First published in paperback 2000
Reprinted 2000 (twice), 2001, 2002 (twice), 2004 (twice)
© Ainsley Harriott 1997
The moral right of Ainsley Harriott to be identified as the author
of this work has been asserted.

ISBN 0 563 38366 6 (hardback)
ISBN 0 563 55181 X (paperback)

Recipes developed and written in
association with Debbie Major.
Designed by the Senate
Studio photographs by Gus Filgate
Location photographs by Craig Easton
Home Economist: Maxine Clarke
Stylist: Helen Payne

Printed and bound in Great Britain by Butler and Tanner Ltd, Frome
Colour origination by Radstock Reproductions Ltd, Midsomer Norton

Ainsley Harriott's Barbecue Bible

CONTENTS

Welcome to a whole new world
of barbecue food.
Hua Hin Beach, Thailand.

INTRODUCTION

I've always wanted to write a book on barbecuing that would make everyone instantly comfortable and confident for when the barbie season sets in (weather permitting). Surely, there's absolutely no better feeling than cooking and eating '*al fresco*'. Some say it's the ultimate cooking experience, and who am I to disagree? Once you've captured the art of barbecuing even novice cooks can achieve superb results and delicious aromas whilst strutting their stuff over the coals.

My travels have taken me all over the world and I've discovered that some countries still use barbecuing as their basic means of cooking, although all have developed their own technique, style and distinctive flavouring. The flavour imparted to barbecued food by the ingredients of a particular region adds to the flavour that the food absorbs from the smoke produced by the glistening, dripping cooking juices to produce a very individual taste. I've gained some invaluable information which I can share with you.

Cooking over coals or an open fire has been practised for hundreds of years, in fact since prehistoric man, yet today the technique remains essentially the same. Now we have lots of wonderful ingredients at our disposal, although the loin cloth has been replaced by designer shorts, shirts and skirts. But like our prehistoric brothers and sisters, you can't beat finger-lickin' food. It's deliciously sociable.

So... let's forget the days of burnt chicken or charred bangers and burgers. The *Barbecue Bible* will make you into a connoisseur of the coals. Go on, get sizzling!

BARBECUE INFORMATION

Whether you are an occasional or a regular barbecuer, there are a wide range of barbecues to choose from, ranging from the small disposable trays to the most sophisticated grills set in glamorous trolleys with table attachments and all the gadgets. Here are some hints and guidelines on what to look out for.

WHICH TYPE OF BARBECUE DO YOU CHOOSE?

There are two basic types of barbecue available – charcoal or gas – and whichever type you choose, they both work on the same basic principles.

The food is placed on a rack over the heat and as it cooks, it releases melted fat and cooking juices. These fall off on to the heat source (charcoal, coals, lava rocks or metal bars or plates) which converts this moisture into smoke which then rises up and flavours the food. Contrary to popular belief, charcoal in itself imparts no actual flavour – it is only the smoke from the cooking juices and any aromatics added to the coals which actually add any flavour to the food – so you do, in fact, get that same outdoor flavour when you use gas too.

THINGS TO LOOK OUT FOR WHEN BUYING A BARBECUE

GENERAL POINTS

Buy your barbecue from a well-known, trusted manufacturer who offers a good warranty as well as replacement parts and products.

Choose a barbecue appropriate to your needs, depending on whether you barbecue just once or twice a year or regularly throughout the summer, and even winter. Also if you wish to take your barbecue out and about with you – to the beach, on a picnic or when you go camping – buy one which is compact and easy to transport.

Take storage space for a dormant barbecue into account. Some of the larger ones will require garage or shed space when not in use.

Buy a barbecue which is made to last and which will withstand corrosion and remain rust-free. The slightly more expensive ones will be better made and will last up to five times longer than the cheaper models.

Take the assembly of your new barbecue into account. Ask your dealer how easy or difficult it is to put together and roughly how long it will take – obviously, the more elaborate your barbecue, the more parts it will have, but clear, precise instructions are essential. Also check that the parts are precision-made so that they fit together well and easily, and make sure that there are no sharp, unrolled edges anywhere.

Check out the stability of the assembled barbecue because this is a very important safety aspect. Are the legs in proportion to the size of the hearth and thick and sturdy enough to withstand the weight of the barbecue once it is laden with hot coals and food? Also, will it be sturdy and wobble-free once in use? If the barbecue is set in a trolley with wheels, are they rugged enough to withstand the weight of the barbecue and the terrain when moving it into position?

Choose a barbecue which will offer you adequate primary cooking space for the number of people you wish to cater for on a regular basis. This means the actual cooking area over the coals rather than any racks or warming shelves. More overall square inches does not always provide more cooking space. Those barbecues with stacked grills and warming racks may seem convenient and offer lots more space but they are often lacking when it comes to the practicalities of cooking.

Make sure that the cooking racks are in proportion to the size of the cooking area and are sturdy enough so that they do not sag under the weight of the food that the area can accommodate. Also check that the bars are not spaced too far apart or your food will be forever falling down between them. Slightly thicker bars will also sear a larger area of the food, giving it a more 'barbecued' flavour. Some racks are porcelain-enamelled which will prevent the food sticking during cooking and prevent rusting when not in use but they are a little more heavy and do stand the chance of chipping if you don't look after them.

The handles on any barbecue should be made of wood or cool-to-the-touch plastic, not metal. If you would like the option of cooking larger joints of meat on your barbecue, choose one with a lid which is large enough to accommodate a joint.

With the more fancy models, make sure that the table attachments are easy to clean as well as heat and weather resistant.

CHARCOAL BARBECUES

There are those people who enjoy the fun of this more primitive, traditional style of cooking which involves the hands-on activity of building and regulating a natural fire (you little cave person, you!).

There is a wider price range of charcoal barbecues available, from the very cheap disposable trays to the more sophisticated models as well as a bigger range of small or portable barbecues which enable you to cook in restricted spaces such as on balconies and in small gardens, or while at the beach, camping and on holiday and so on. If you choose to cook on charcoal, you have the option of constructing a barbecue yourself from bricks or rocks and a rack wherever and whenever you wish. If you are buying a cast-iron barbecue, buy one made from virgin solid cast iron. These will have the ability to reach and withstand higher temperatures, will diffuse the heat more evenly and efficiently and will retain the heat for longer. Recycled cast iron contains impurities, bubbles and cracks which might not withstand such high temperatures and could prove dangerous. If you are buying a steel barbecue, buy one made from heavy-gauge steel sealed with porcelain enamel which will be able to withstand the high cooking temperatures and make it easier to clean up afterwards.

Choose between an open grate or a covered grill. A grill with a hood will offer you more options on how the food can be cooked, but make sure there are sufficient air vents to allow maximum air flow. About three in the base and one in the lid is ideal.

Choose a barbecue which is easy to clean according to its size. Tipping the ashes out of a small, portable barbecue should pose no problems but this would be far more difficult with the much larger models. Specially designed ash collectors will make life a lot easier.

GAS BARBECUES

These grills are convenient and ready for use at the drop of a hat.

They will light at the touch of a button and will be ready to cook on in about 10 minutes, much faster than charcoal. You also have better control over the temperature of your barbecue with gas. They are relatively inexpensive to operate, easy to use and quick to clean up and store away after use.

Try to avoid barbecues with glass windows in the lid if you can. They serve no purpose, blacken very quickly and are very hard to clean. When the lids are closed they tend to reflect the heat unevenly and can sometimes shatter under high temperatures.

Check that the gas burners in the base of the hearth are made from stainless steel, not aluminized steel. An H shaped burner will give you more heat coverage. They also need to be shielded from the drippings so that they do not become clogged up during use. Individual controls for each burner will offer you more versatility, enabling you to cook by the direct or indirect method of cooking (see page 14).

Make sure that it is easy to connect and remove the gas tanks before and after use. An accurate gauge indicating the level of fuel in the tank is useful so that it doesn't run out during cooking. A rubber connecting hose is also better than a plastic one.

Check out the type and location of the ignition systems. A convenient, easy-to-use push-button system makes life a lot easier.

Ask questions about the fuel consumption of gas barbecues. Some models claim to have good heat outputs but when you use them go through a tank of gas like it's going out of fashion. Look out for one with the most efficient system.

**OVERLEAF Sucking one of the local specialities.
Chatuchak Market, Bangkok.**

THE TYPES OF CHARCOAL AND GAS BARBECUES AVAILABLE

CHARCOAL BARBECUES

Disposable barbecues

These are now readily available in most supermarkets, department stores and DIY shops, especially during the summer months. They consist of shallow foil trays filled with charcoal and a sheet of firelighting paper.

They are cheap and portable, ideal for smaller spaces especially balconies, and are very easy to light. The only disadvantages are that they do not offer that much primary cooking area (although they do stay hot for an amazingly long time so you could cook more food in rotation if you wished) and the rack is very close to the coals which means that they are only really suitable for cooking smaller, thinner pieces of food such as burgers, chops, sausages and kebabs. Larger, thicker pieces of food would blacken too much on the outside before being properly cooked in the middle.

They can either be set on the ground or placed at table-top height on a heat-resistant surface.

Hibachi barbecues

These are shallow, trough-like, portable barbecues, originating from Japan, which stand on very short legs and can be set on the ground or on a heat-resistant surface at table-top height. They have two vertical, notched rungs set on one long side of the hearth into which the cooking rack can be locked, enabling you to adjust the distance of the foods from the coals depending on the cooking time required. These are not really suitable for cooking larger joints of meat.

Convertible barbecues

These simple, portable, cast-iron barbecues have an L-shaped hearth which can be used in the traditional way, with the hot coals sitting beneath the horizontal cooking rack. However, they can also be rotated by 90° so that the coals produce a vertical back-burner in front of which a spike can be positioned for spit roasting. They can be either positioned on the ground or at table-top height.

Upright open-top barbecues

These come in all shapes and sizes and simply consist of an open hearth without a lid, either supported on legs or set into a simple trolley with wheels. Once they are assembled they require somewhere for storage when not in use. Plastic covers are available but they do not really offer long-term protection. They can only be used for the direct method of cooking and offer no protection from strong winds.

Barrel barbecues

These look like little pot-bellied stoves and they offer a very attractive, stable, open-top style barbecue at table-top height. They are made from cast iron and have adjustable cooking racks and often stands for accommodating rotisserie spits. The main advantage with them is that their unique design makes them very easy to light and quick to reach cooking temperature, unlike most other charcoal barbecues which can take up to 45 minutes. Newspaper or kindling is placed underneath the charcoal grate which is then replaced and covered with the charcoal. The air vent in the side of the barbecue is opened and the kindling or newspaper is lit, which ignites the charcoal so quickly that is ready to cook on in just 10–15 minutes.

Pillar or pedestal barbecues

These consist of a hearth set on a thick tube-like pedestal and they work in a similar way to the barrel barbecues. The pillar is packed with newspaper and the coals are arranged in the hearth above. The paper is lit with a taper via a hole in the pillar which quickly lights the charcoal above.

Covered kettle barbecues

These come in various sizes, offering a range of primary cooking areas as well as other accessories such as ash catchers, various cleaning systems and built-in thermometers. There are small, portable barbecues which are ideal for picnics and balconies, free-standing models, and then those that are mounted in trolleys with added extras such as fuel storage bins and gas ignition systems. Not only can they be used for the more traditional direct method of cooking (see page 14) (as with an open-top barbecue), but they also have rounded lids which will enable you to cook by the indirect method (see page 14), where they will act like conventional ovens when the lid is closed. The heat from the coals is reflected evenly around the foods, reducing the cooking times, sealing in the juices and enhancing that smoky 'barbecue' flavour, as well as removing oxygen from the cooking surface, eliminating the possibility of flare-ups which are caused when the fatty cooking juices fall into the fire.

Hooded barbecues

These are generally large rectangular barbecues with hinged lids which are set into movable trolleys. They work in the same way as the kettle barbecues and are often available with extras such as movable grates, rotisseries, warming racks, side tables, separate burners for side dishes and so on.

Permanent brick barbecues

Some companies now offer do-it-yourself kits which enable you to construct your own permanent barbecue in your garden. Strong metal pegs are mounted in a three-sided brick wall which support a solid plate for the coals and a large metal rack above. These are ideal for people who do a lot of barbecuing because they provide lots of primary cooking space and they are always available for use whenever the mood takes you.

GAS BARBECUES
Portable barbecues

These can be small round or rectangular hooded barbecues with short legs which sometimes swing up and over the lid to lock it in place during transport. They run on small disposable gas cylinders which heat either lava rocks or flat flavourizing bars or plates. These are ideal for picnics, beach parties and camping holidays and for people with very little storage space who like to do a little barbecuing every now and then.

Table height barbecues

These are always set into table-height trolley units usually with wheels which means that they can be easily manoeuvred into place before use. They range from the most simple of trolleys with perhaps one small side table, right up to those with sometimes half the cooking area given over to a solid griddle plate, rotisseries, thermometers, smoker units, baking ovens, racks for holding cooking oils and sauces, enclosed shelved cupboards below and side-burners for side dishes and sauces.

ELECTRIC BARBECUES

These barbecues are available in small table-top sizes or larger table-height models and are heated by an electric element positioned under the rack. They act more like a domestic grill in reverse (with the heat coming from underneath) and the main disadvantage is that they either need to be used near a power point or will require a long extension lead.

FUELS

The secret to a good barbecue is a good fire. The art of achieving this, controlling the heat and distributing it evenly comes with practice, but you will need the right fuel before you can begin.

WOOD

Dry hardwood can be used for barbecuing foods but it is more difficult to start and the fire will not last as long as either charcoal or briquettes. This is best for hand-built, impromptu barbecues.

CHARCOAL

There are two main types of fuel for a charcoal barbecue; one is lumpwood charcoal and the other is charcoal briquettes.

Lumpwood charcoal

This is not a fossilized fuel extracted from the ground as some people would believe, but is in fact wood which has been fired in a kiln.

This process cooks the wood without igniting it and drives out all the by-products, leaving behind a very light, black, combustible form of carbon.

Good-quality charcoal normally gives you larger pieces which will make your barbecuing much easier.

The 'green issue'

Charcoal requires trees for its manufacture and with the increasing popularity in this method of cooking all over the world, the demand on the world's forests is increasing. In the past few years, charcoal production has been a contributing factor to the deforestation of the tropical rainforests because it has been unregulated, but now an international organization called the FSC (Forest Stewardship Council), sponsored by the Worldwide Fund for Nature has been set up to monitor and regulate the use of trees from selected areas of forests. Charcoal with the FSC logo is now available in most of the UK's large retail outlets.

Instant lighting lumpwood charcoal

This is a very convenient form of charcoal which has been impregnated with a lighting agent. About 1 kg (2¼ lb) of fuel is sold in a sealed paper bag which is simply placed in the hearth and then lit with a match, therefore removing the need for firelighters or lighting fluids. Once this charcoal is alight, more fuel can be added to the hearth if necessary to give you a bigger bed of coals.

Charcoal briquettes

These are uniformly shaped lumps of fuel which are made from particles of waste charcoal mixed with a starch binder. Once lit, these tend to burn for longer than lumpwood charcoal.

Other barbecue fuels

Some cheaper barbecue briquettes are made from alternative sources of fuel, filled out with things like sand, sawdust and anthracite, all bound together with a petroleum-based substance. For good, 'natural' barbecuing, it is better to choose a quality briquette made from pure lumpwood charcoal.

GAS

These can be run on either LP (Liquid Petroleum) gas or natural gas. LP gas is available in two forms: butane, which generally comes in a blue cylinder, or propane, which comes in a red cylinder. It is best to use propane gas in cold weather as it operates at a lower temperature than butane. Natural gas is not available in Europe in cylinder form. Special fittings which can be attached to the outside wall of the house will draw gas from the main supply and can be connected to the barbecue when required. The disadvantage with this system is that the barbecue needs to be used near to the house.

FIRELIGHTERS

There are a number of different ways of lighting a charcoal barbecue.

Barbecue firelighters

These waxy-looking cubes or sticks are specially designed to light barbecues without giving off any fumes which will taint the food. A recommended number are simply pushed in amongst the charcoal or briquettes and then lit with a match. As they stay alight for quite a few minutes, they give time for the charcoal to ignite and they are clean, very safe and easy to use. It is important not to use other types of firelighters which are designed for lighting domestic grate-style fires. These contain paraffin which could badly taint the food.

Firelighter fluids

This is a commonly used product for lighting a barbecue which is odourless, clean and safe in the proper hands. It is very dangerous if used incorrectly and should never be squirted directly on to a burning fire as the flame could travel back up to the bottle in a split second. Pour a little of the firelighter fluid on to the dry fuel and leave it to soak in for 2–3 minutes. Then light it with a taper or long safety match.

Firelighter gels

This is a relatively new product on the market. This thick, sticky gel is squeezed on to the fuel and then set alight. However, great care must be taken not to get it on to the fingers in case it catches alight when you go to ignite the barbecue which could result in a nasty burn.

Electric starters

These are flat, looped heating elements attached to a handle and an electric cable. They are placed in amongst the coals, switched on and left until the coals catch fire. The disadvantage of these is you will need an electric power point nearby.

FIRE AROMATICS

Barbecued foods can be given a more distinctive flavour by adding either natural or manufactured flavourings to the fire just before cooking.

- Dry twigs from fruit trees and vine cuttings can be added to a charcoal barbecue.
- The woody stalks and leaves of some fresh herbs such as rosemary, thyme or bay can be added to a charcoal barbecue.
- Leftover almond, walnut and hazelnut shells which have been soaked in water for 30 minutes can be sprinkled on to a charcoal barbecue.
- Soaked dried seaweed can be added to a charcoal barbecue when cooking fish and shellfish.
- Small chips, made from old whisky barrels or hickory, mesquite, oak, apple or plum wood can be used on either charcoal or gas barbecues. The loose chips should be soaked in cold water for 30 minutes beforehand and can be sprinkled directly on to a charcoal barbecue just before cooking. For gas barbecues they should be rolled up into a foil sausage, pierced here and there with a skewer and then rested on the lava rocks or flavourizer bars.

Types of Charcoal Barbecues Available

1. Pillar or Pedestal Barbecue
2. Covered Kettle Barbecue
3. Barrel Barbecue
4. Hibachi Barbecue

❶

❸

❷

❹

GETTING THINGS READY

Place your barbecue on a level surface away from trees, fences, hedges, etc. If it is windy, try and find somewhere a bit more sheltered.

Allow at least 45 minutes for a charcoal barbecue to reach the correct cooking temperature. A gas barbecue is probably ready to cook on in about 10 minutes.

Remove any chilled meats from the fridge and allow them to come back to room temperature.

Make sure that everything else is ready, so that once the barbecue has reached the right temperature you can start cooking and serve up straight away.

COOKING ON A CHARCOAL BARBECUE

LIGHTING THE BARBECUE

Do not be tempted to fill the hearth with charcoal in the hope of making a fire which will last longer and cook better. It is simply a waste of fuel and the fire will become too hot to cook on anyway.

Remove the lid if there is one and open all the vents. Spread the charcoal or briquettes two layers deep over the base of the barbecue. Scoop it back up into a pyramid and tuck in the firelighters if using.

Light the firelighters and leave until the coals start to glow red (5–10 minutes). Rake the coals back out into an even layer and leave until they have reached the required temperature (30–45 minutes).

COOKING TEMPERATURES
Hot

The flames will have disappeared and coals will be glowing red and be coved with a light dusting of white ash. You should only be able to hold your hand about 15 cm (6 in) away from the coals for about 2 seconds. This temperature is only suitable for very thin pieces of food such as chicken escalopes, fish fillets and chipolata sausages.

Medium hot

The coals should now be covered with a thicker layer of white ash and you should be able to hold you hand above the fire for about 5 seconds.

This temperature is suitable for most barbecued foods.

Cool

The coals should now no longer be glowing red and should be covered in a very thick layer of ash. You should be able to hold your hand over the fire for about 8 seconds. This temperature is fine for foods that simply need warming through rather than cooking, such as fresh fruit parcels.

You can also alter the temperature by moving the food closer or further away from the heat (obviously, the closer it is, the hotter it will be and vice versa) and it will also depend on whether the food is placed directly over the coals or pushed to the side of the rack away from the hottest part of the fire.

Regulating the Temperature

To increase the temperature of the fire a little, knock some of the ash off the coals and push them a little closer together.

To cool the barbecue down, spread out the coals a little and partly close any vents.

If you need to cook on the barbecue for any more than 45 minutes to 1 hour you will need to add more coals. Either push the coals together and add new ones around the edge or alternatively light a new batch of coals in a second barbecue or a large metal roasting tin as soon as the first lot are ready and transfer them to the cooling fire with metal tongs.

METHODS OF COOKING

DIRECT COOKING

This is where the food is placed on a rack directly over a solid area of heat (a bed of hot coals or a gas burner). The barbecue can be used uncovered or covered. The foods need to be turned so that both sides become cooked and they can be seared over the hottest part of the fire in the centre of the rack and then moved to the edge to finish cooking through. This method is ideal for cooking things that require up to 45 minutes cooking time.

INDIRECT COOKING

This is where the heat source is restricted to the edges of the hearth, leaving a space clear in the centre for the food and a drip tray. This is only possible on a lidded barbecue. With charcoal barbecues the coals are placed on opposite sides of the hearth and with gas barbecues with dual burners, the middle burner closest to the food is turned off. The food is placed on the rack directly above the drip tray and then the lid is lowered into place. Because heat is reflected off the lid as well as coming from underneath the barbecue almost acts like a conventional oven which means that the food doesn't need to be turned during cooking. This method is ideal for cooking larger joints of meat like whole chickens and legs of lamb. When using this method, try not to lift the lid too often because a lot of heat is lost this way. Add a little extra cooking time to compensate for each time you take a peek at the food.

SPIT ROASTING

Some charcoal and gas barbecues either have the ability to accommodate spit roasting attachments or they come with them already supplied. The meat is skewered onto the spit rod and held in place on either side with two adjustable spit forks. The rod is suspended over the heat (it is sometimes necessary to remove the rack first so that the food has enough room in which to turn) and the food is left to rotate slowly, powered by either a battery or electrically driven motor.

SAFETY GUIDELINES

- Always read the manufacturers instructions carefully before assembling and using a new barbecue.
- Always set a barbecue on a firm, level surface away from anything which could catch fire such as fences, trees, hedges, etc.
- Always place portable barbecues on a heatproof surface or the ground.
- Never try to start a barbecue in high winds.
- Never use a barbecue indoors unless it has been specially designed for this purpose.
- Always open the lid of a gas barbecue before lighting.
- Once the barbecue is alight, never leave it unattended and keep children and animals away from it.
- Never use charcoal on a gas barbecue. Charcoal burns very hot and in most cases will melt the shell of a gas barbecue. Also, charcoal burns to ash which would mix with the cooking fats and clog up the gas burners.
- Never light a barbecue with paraffin, petrol or white spirit. Not only is this extremely dangerous but it would also taint the food and render it inedible. Use only purpose-branded firelighters and fuels and follow the manufacturers instructions carefully.

- Keep matches well away from a lit barbecue.
- Never attempt to move a barbecue once lit.
- With a gas barbecue, always check that the gas regulator is appropriate for the barbecue. Also check that the gas hose has not perished or cracked in any way and that it is properly connected to the barbecue and the gas cylinder before lighting.
- Dress sensibly when cooking on a barbecue. Try to avoid long loose clothing and wear an apron to avoid burns from spitting fats etc.
- Always leave a barbecue to cool down completely before cleaning it and packing it away. This can take several hours.
- Never try to extinguish a barbecue by pouring cold water on to it. There is the possibility that the metal hearth could contract and crack and porcelain-enamelled surfaces may shatter.

CLEANING UP A BARBECUE

CHARCOAL BARBECUES

Remove the cooking rack once cold and scrub off as much residue as you can with a wire brush or crumpled piece of foil. Then wash it with an abrasive soap-filled scouring pad. It might be necessary to use an oven cleaner too, every once in a while. If you look after the rack it will give you better service for much longer.

Remove the cold ashes from the hearth and brush out the fine dust.

Every once in a while, clean the rest of the barbecue with an oven cleaner to get rid of any accumulated greases and dirt. Rinse thoroughly, and make sure it is completely dry before you pack it away.

GAS BARBECUES

Always clean the rack, lid, any drip trays, gas burners, etc. before packing it away.

Lava rocks can be cleaned a couple of times during their life to get rid of old cooking fats and juices. Wash them in hot soapy water, rinse and leave to dry. However, they do need to be replaced every now and then, otherwise old cooking juices etc. can flavour the new food next time you use it.

Give the outside of the barbecue a good wash with warm soapy water now and then to keep it looking nice and help it last longer.

BARBECUE EQUIPMENT

ESSENTIAL
- Long-handled tongs, spatulas and forks are essential for turning foods and removing them from the cooking rack.
- A long-handled basting brush is essential for brushing glazes on to partly cooked meats.
- Oven mitts are a must for removing kebabs etc. from the barbecue.
- You will need an assortment of skewers. Long, flat metal skewers are ideal for chunkier meat and fish kebabs and for holding spatchcocked poultry and butterflied joints of meat flat during cooking. Long and short bamboo skewers are ideal for smaller, more delicate foods which require shorter cooking times. Small, fine, metal trussing skewers are great for sealing in stuffings and holding rolled foods together during cooking. Cocktail sticks will do a similar job.

NON-ESSENTIAL BUT USEFUL
- Hinged wire racks are available for barbecuing large individual fish, more than one smaller fish, sausages, burgers and kebabs, etc. They make it much easier and quicker to turn the food over during cooking and help to prevent it from sticking to the rack.
- Fine wire mesh racks which rest on the bars of the main cooking rack are useful for cooking smaller items of food which would otherwise fall through the bars.
- A wire brush and scraper makes the job of cleaning up the cooking rack a lot easier and is also useful for quickly removing larger pieces of stuck on food from the rack during cooking.
- A meat thermometer will help you to test the internal temperature of larger joints of meat.

OTHER POSSIBLE ATTACHMENTS AND ACCESSORIES
- Specially designed kebab racks enable you to suspend half a dozen skewers over the heat at once. As they do not come into contact with the rack during cooking, there is no problem with the kebabs sticking and they are also much easier to turn.
- Some barbecues enable you to attach a battery or electrically driven rotisserie which is great for cooking whole chickens and larger joints of meat.
- Plastic covers for both charcoal and gas barbecues will help protect them from dust and debris while they are in storage, and out of doors from the weather in the short term.

Useful Barbecue Equipment

1. **Basting Brush**
2. **Long-handled Spatula**
3. **Long-handled Fork**
4. **Long-handled Tongs**
5. **Fine Wire Mesh Rack**
6. **Long Metal Skewers**
7. **Single Fish Rack**
8. **Hinged Wire Rack for Sausages, Burgers, etc.**

AINSLEY'S KITCHEN TIPS

To help you on your way, here are a few guidelines on how to do some of the cooking techniques referred to in the recipes.

To finely chop onions or shallots. Peel the onion, leaving the root end intact. Sit your onion root-side down on a chopping board and thinly slice through the onion almost down to the root. The closer together you make the cuts, the finer your finished dice will be. Slice the onion in half through the middle cut, lay it flat-side down on the board and thinly cut up towards the root again. Now slice across the onion and it will miraculously fall away in neat little pieces. Throw away the root end.

To skin, seed and dice a tomato. Cover the tomato in boiling water and leave for 30 seconds. Drain, cover with cold water and when cool enough to handle, peel off the skin. Cut it into quarters, discard the seeds and finely chop the flesh.

To seed and chop a fresh chilli. Some people like to wear rubber gloves to do this job. If not, you have to be careful not to touch your eyes, mouth, etc. for a while afterwards. You can simply cut them in half lengthways and then scoop out the seeds with a teaspoon so that you don't touch the seeds, which are the most fiery bit. Then you just need to chop the flesh finely. You can of course leave the seeds in if you like things extra hot.

To pare the zest off a lemon or lime. Thinly peel off the coloured part of the skin using a really sharp potato peeler, making sure you don't take off too much of the bitter white pith underneath with it.

Chopping herbs. You can of course do this on a chopping board with a sharp knife but a crafty little trick is to pack the herbs loosely in a coffee mug and chop around inside the mug with a pair of scissors until they are done to your liking.

Peeling garlic cloves. A nifty way of quickly getting the papery skin off the outside of a garlic clove is to place it on a board and very lightly crush it under the blade of a large kitchen knife. The skin will drop off just like magic.

Extracting the juice from a piece of fresh root ginger. Peel the piece of ginger and then grate it on the finest side of your grater straight on to a small plate. Scrape out all the bits from the inside of the grater and then collect it all up into a ball. Squeeze the pulp into another bowl and you will be amazed at how much juice comes out. The juice is great for making sauces and marinades without getting little bits of ginger in them. Discard the leftover fibrous material.

Chopping a stalk of lemongrass. I find that it is best to remove at least one layer of the leaves from the outside of the stalk before you start because they can be a bit woody. If it is going to be ground into a paste in a food processor you can just trim off the end and finely chop the rest of the stalk but if you want to add it to a sauce in little pieces, pull off another layer of leaves until you reach the tender central core before chopping.

To roast whole spices. This brings out all the wonderful flavour of the spices. Heat a dry, heavy-based frying pan over a high heat until it is really quite hot. Add the spices and shake the pan over the heat until they start to smell aromatic and have darkened very slightly. You can now either grind them up in a pestle and mortar or electric coffee grinder, or leave them whole.

To sterilize bottles and jars. Wash them out in soapy hot water and rinse them thoroughly. Dry them in a warm oven set at 140°C/275°F/Gas mark 1, then remove and leave to cool.

To make fresh white breadcrumbs. Remove the crusts from slices of fresh white bread and whizz them around in a food processor for a couple of minutes until they have broken down into crumbs.

To toast pine kernels and other nuts. Spread them over a shallow baking tray and slide them under a hot grill or into a hot oven and cook for a few minutes, shaking the tray every now and then, until they are lightly browned all over. Watch them like a hawk though – they can burn in a matter of seconds!

All the spoon measurements in this book are level unless otherwise stated. A tablespoon is 15 ml; a teaspoon is 5 ml.

Follow one set of measurements when following any of the recipes. Do not mix metric with imperial.

All the ingredients in the recipes are listed with the most important ingredient first, followed by the other ingredients in order of use. This will make things easier for you when you are following the recipes.

AINSLEY'S BARBECUING TIPS

Do not leave raw food out in the sun before cooking. Keep it cool (but at room temperature) and covered until you are ready to cook it.

Try not to pack food on to a skewer too tightly. Leave some gaps around each piece so that they can cook through thoroughly.

Always soak bamboo and wooden skewers in water for about 30 minutes before using or they will catch fire during cooking.

Flat metal skewers for kebabs help to stop the food from spinning around as you turn them. A good trick is to thread the food on to pairs of parallel skewers which will hold it firmly in place.

Lightly brush the cooking rack with a little oil before cooking. This should help prevent food from sticking to it.

Try to scrape most of the marinade off the food before grilling as this is what causes the coals to flare up during cooking.

Only baste food with a sugary glaze during the last 10 minutes or so of cooking, otherwise it tends to burn.

When cooking in a foil parcel, always use an extra-thick, heavy-duty foil.

Have a spray bottle of water handy to put out any flames as they appear.

BARBECUE BASICS

MARINADES, RUBS & SAUCES

In this section of the book I have given lots of ideas on how to flavour fish and meats before or during cooking and a selection of butters, salsas, sauces and relishes to serve up on the side.

For some very simple barbecue recipes, all you have to do is first choose which type of fish or meat you wish to cook, decide on how you want to flavour it, if at all, look at the cooking chart (pages 38–9) to see how long you will need to cook it and then choose something to serve with it. However, don't be tempted to try something from each section for everything that you cook otherwise the flavours will get too complicated.

Simply grilled meats and fish will often taste just as nice with one of the savoury butters or a spoonful of one of the salsas, for example, so try to mix and match things quite carefully.

MARINADES

These are mostly oil-based mixtures used to flavour and tenderize fish and meats prior to cooking and to help keep them moist during cooking.

It is very important to remember not to overdo the oil in a marinade as this is what causes a barbecue to flare up, resulting in that well-known blackened barbecue look.

- All these marinades are sufficient for 900 g (2 lb) of meat or fish.
- Make shallow cuts over the surface of the fish or meat before marinating if you wish. It will help the flavours to penetrate right into the food.
- Pour the marinade into a shallow, non-metallic dish, large enough to carry the food in one layer, and remember to give it a turn every now and then while it is marinating.
- Marinate red meats, poultry and game for 2 hours at room temperature or 24–48 hours in the fridge.
- Marinate fish, seafood and vegetables somewhere cool for 30 minutes or up to 2 hours in the fridge.
- Bring chilled foods back to room temperature before cooking.
- Scrape most of the excess marinade off the food before cooking to prevent the barbecue from flaring up.

Tomato and Chilli Marinade

Go on, give your meat a spicy treat. This goes particularly well with chicken, pork, lamb or beef.

2 tablespoons sunflower oil
2 tablespoons red wine vinegar
2 tablespoons tomato purée
2 tablespoons minced red chilli from a jar
1 tablespoon Worcestershire sauce
2 teaspoons caster sugar
salt and freshly ground black pepper

Mix all the ingredients together and use as required.

Barbecue tuna and sweet potato
chips – best catch of the day.
Paternoster Beach, South Africa.

Indian Yoghurt Marinade

If you like it cool and spicy, this is a wonderful marinade for chicken, lamb and firm white fish such as cod or monkfish.

8 tablespoons natural yoghurt
3 garlic cloves, crushed
2.5 cm (1 in) fresh root ginger, peeled and finely grated
juice of ½ lemon
2 teaspoons ground turmeric
4 green cardamom pods, lightly crushed
1 teaspoon ground cumin
1 teaspoon ground coriander
¼ teaspoon cayenne pepper
½ teaspoon salt

Mix all the ingredients together and use as required.

Moroccan Spiced Marinade

This is great for chicken, lamb and steaks. If you like it hot, hot, hot, add an extra teaspoon of harissa paste.

1 tablespoon olive oil
juice of 2 small lemons
1 teaspoon ground cumin
¼ teaspoon ground cinnamon
pinch of ground cloves
½ teaspoon ground turmeric
1 teaspoon harissa paste or minced red chilli from a jar
1 small onion, very finely chopped
2 garlic cloves, crushed
salt and freshly ground black pepper

Mix all the ingredients together and use as required.

Greek Garlic, Lemon and Oregano Marinade

This is wonderful with lamb, chicken and stronger-flavoured fish such as swordfish and would also work well with vegetables or cubes of haloumi and black olives on soaked bamboo skewers. You could use 1 tablespoon of chopped fresh thyme in place of the oregano if you wish.

2 garlic cloves, crushed
finely grated zest and juice of 1 lemon
2 tablespoons chopped fresh oregano
1 teaspoon clear honey
4 tablespoons olive oil
salt and freshly ground black pepper

Mix all the ingredients together and use as required.

Chinese Marinade

This one is so simple and the ingredients are easy to get. It's especially good with pork and chicken.

2.5 cm (1 in) piece fresh root ginger, peeled
4 tablespoons dark soy sauce
2 tablespoons white wine vinegar
1 tablespoon dry sherry
pinch of caster sugar
4 garlic cloves, very finely chopped
2 tablespoons clear honey
1 teaspoon five-spice powder

Finely grate the ginger, collect it up into a ball and squeeze out the juice into a bowl.
Stir in the other ingredients and use as required.

Fennel and Lemon Marinade

This is ideal for delicately flavoured white fish and seafood. Fennel herb is not always easy to come by, so just substitute another herb with a slightly aniseed flavour such as tarragon or basil if need be.

1 tablespoon fennel seeds, crushed
3 tablespoons chopped fresh fennel herb, tarragon or basil
finely grated zest and juice of 1 small lemon
4 tablespoons olive oil
2 garlic cloves, crushed
salt and freshly ground black pepper

Mix all the ingredients together and use as required.

Thai Spiced Marinade

Now here's a trendy marinade that really gets the tastebuds buzzing. It goes really well with any meat or firm white fish.

200 ml (7 fl oz) canned coconut milk
2 tablespoons Thai fish sauce
juice of 1 lime
2 kaffir lime leaves, very finely shredded or finely grated zest of 1 lime
1 stalk lemongrass, outer leaves discarded and core very finely chopped
4 cm (1½ in) fresh root ginger, peeled and very finely grated
2 red or green finger chillies, seeded and very finely chopped
2 spring onions, trimmed and very thinly sliced
salt and freshly ground black pepper

Mix all the ingredients together in a bowl and set aside for 2 hours to allow the flavours to infuse before using as required.

See also:

Yakitori marinade, Yakitori Skewers page 51
Green Thai curry paste marinade, Coco-Chicken and Mango Skewers page 64
Rum and sugar marinade, Uncle's Pork Calypso page 66
Teriyaki marinade, Chinese Lattice Pork page 67
Chinese red roast pork marinade, Char Sui Lettuce Rolls page 68
North African harissa and spice marinade, Moroccan Spiced Lamb Kebabs page 72
Mexican tequila and spice marinade, Mighty Mexican Lamb or Beef Fajitas page 74
Masala marinade, Mari-Masala Lamb Fillets page 75
Red wine marinade, Beef 'Bourguignon' Kebabs page 82
Sweet chilli marinade, Sweet Chilli King Prawns page 104
Citrus marinade, Citrus Seafood Kebabs page 107

SPICE AND HERB RUBS

Now we all like a good rub, so here's something else which you can put on to the outside of your food before barbecuing to help give it a different flavour. A spice rub is simply a different combination of dried spices ground together into a fine powder. They can either be put directly on to the meat or mixed into a paste with a little oil before using and they will give a deliciously crisp, drier finish to all types of barbecued meats and fish. Any leftover mixtures can be stored in an airtight container for later use, but they will gradually lose their intensity of flavour, so it's better if you can make them up just before you use them.

Herb rubs are a mixture of fresh herbs and spices, blended to a paste with a little oil and lemon juice. These will not keep so well so they will need to be used as soon as they are made.

- All the spice and herb rubs are sufficient to coat 900 g (2 lb) of meat, poultry or fish.
- Remove the skin from chicken before adding the dry or wet rub.
- If you wish, make shallow cuts over the surface of the fish or meat before adding the rub so that the flavours can penetrate right into the food.
- Cover the meat or fish with the spice or herb rub and set aside for at least 1 hour before cooking.

Barbecue Spice Rub

This is perfect for all meats, especially chicken, and when cooking on the barbie, gives off the most delightful of aromas.

2 teaspoons paprika (hot or mild)
2 teaspoons dried chilli flakes
2 teaspoons caster sugar
2 teaspoons light soft brown sugar
1 teaspoon ground cumin
1 teaspoon cayenne pepper
2 teaspoons finely ground black pepper
2 teaspoons salt

Simply mix all the ingredients together.

Indian Spiced Rub

This little rub will have them queuing all the way down the road. It goes wonderfully well with chicken, lamb and meaty white fish.

seeds from 12 green cardamom pods
2 teaspoons cayenne pepper
2 teaspoons cumin seeds
2 teaspoons coriander seeds
1 teaspoon black peppercorns
1 teaspoon ground turmeric
1 teaspoon coarse sea salt

Grind all the ingredients to a fine powder in a coffee grinder or a mortar and pestle.

Cajun Spiced Rub

This is the well-known spice mixture used for traditional 'blackened' dishes and really livens up chicken, pork, lamb and meaty types of fish such as swordfish. You should find onion and garlic granules in most supermarkets alongside the other herbs and spices, but be careful not to pick up the flavoured salts by mistake, as they'll make your food too salty. If they don't have granules ask them to get some in. Remember, they want your business.

2 teaspoons hot paprika
1 teaspoon dried thyme
1 teaspoon dried oregano
1 teaspoon black peppercorns
1 teaspoon white peppercorns
1 teaspoon onion granules
1 teaspoon garlic granules
1 teaspoon salt
1 teaspoon cumin seeds

Grind all the ingredients to a fine powder into a coffee grinder or a mortar and pestle.

Mixed Herb and Fennel Rub

You can rub this on your pork and all over your chicken, and even fish likes a good dip in.

2 teaspoons fennel seeds, finely crushed
1 teaspoon coarse sea salt
2 teaspoons chopped fresh rosemary leaves
2 tablespoons chopped fresh flatleaf parsley
1 tablespoon chopped fresh sage
finely grated zest of 2 lemons
3 fat garlic cloves, crushed
2 teaspoons lemon juice
2 tablespoons olive oil
freshly ground black pepper

Mix all the ingredients together and use straight away.

Moroccan Chermoula

This is another paste-like marinade which is superb with all types of fish. Go on, give it that North African ooh la lah.

1½ tablespoons chopped fresh coriander
1½ tablespoons chopped fresh flatleaf parsley
3 garlic cloves, chopped
1 teaspoon ground cumin
1 teaspoon ground coriander
1 red finger chilli, seeded and very finely chopped
2 teaspoons hot paprika (or 1 teaspoon paprika and 1 teaspoon cayenne pepper)
pinch of saffron strands (optional)
finely grated zest and juice of 1 lemon
3 tablespoons extra virgin olive oil
1 teaspoon salt

Put all the ingredients into a food processor and blend to a smooth paste.

OPPOSITE Fennel and Lemon Marinade (see page 22) and Portuguese Piri Piri Glaze (see page 26)

GLAZES

For a sweet, sticky experience, here are some honey- or sugar-based mixtures which will add extra flavour to the outside of your barbecued meats. The sugar slowly caramelizes over the heat to give the meat a deliciously rich, sticky finish. It's best to brush them on half way through or towards the end of cooking because glazes have a tendency to burn if you are not very careful. They are quick to prepare so are generally best made up when you need them. All these glazes are sufficient to coat 900 g (2 lb) meat or poultry.

Portuguese Piri-piri Glaze

This is not exactly an authentic recipe because in Portugal they do not use a sweet chilli sauce, but rather a fiery concoction made from chopped red chillies and lots of salt. Nevertheless, this version tastes fabulous, and although it is traditionally used mainly for chicken and poultry, especially corn-fed ones, there's no reason why you can't use it on other meats too.

2–3 red finger chillies, seeded and very finely
  chopped
6 tablespoons olive oil
3 tablespoons sweet chilli sauce
1 tablespoon dried oregano
salt and freshly ground black pepper

Mix the ingredients together and brush over the meat 10 minutes before the end of cooking.

Yummy Honey, Lime and Ginger Glaze

Get those juices flowing by brushing this delicious glaze over your chicken and pork.

5 cm (2 in) fresh root ginger, peeled
6 tablespoons clear honey
2 tablespoons dry sherry
coarsely grated zest and juice of 1 lime
salt and freshly ground black pepper

Cut the piece of ginger in half. Finely grate one piece, collect it up into a ball and squeeze out the juice into a small bowl.
Cut the rest of the ginger into small strips and stir it into the ginger juice with the rest of the ingredients.
Pour the mixture into a small pan and leave to simmer vigorously for about 3 minutes until reduced by about half.
Leave to cool until thick and syrupy. Brush over the meat 10 minutes before the end of cooking.

Kash and Curry Apple Glaze

Jazz up your chicken, pork, gammon or bacon. This is lip-lickingly good. You will be able to buy concentrated apple juice from any health food shop.

1 tablespoon korma or mild curry paste
2 tablespoons concentrated apple juice
2 tablespoons clear honey
2 tablespoons Dijon mustard
1 tablespoon sieved mango chutney
½ tablespoon cider vinegar
1 clove garlic, crushed
25 g (1 oz) butter

Put all the ingredients into a small pan and stir over a gentle heat until the butter has melted and you have a smooth sauce.
Leave to cool and thicken, then brush over the meat 10 minutes before the end of cooking.

Sweet-n-Spicy Mustard Glaze

This is great for red meats and poultry.

2 tablespoons Dijon mustard
finely grated zest of ½ small orange
¼ teaspoon ground cinnamon
¼ teaspoon ground cloves
3 tablespoons demerara sugar
salt and freshly ground black pepper

Mix all the ingredients together and brush on to the meat 10 minutes before the end of cooking.

Sweet Mint Glossy Glaze

This is wonderful brushed over lamb.

8 tablespoons granulated sugar
250 ml (8 fl oz) water
4 tablespoons chopped fresh mint

Put the sugar and water together into a small pan and stir over a low heat until the sugar has dissolved.
Bring the mixture to the boil and boil vigorously until it has reduced and become quite syrupy.
Remove the pan from the heat and stir in the chopped mint.
Brush on to the meat 10 minutes before the end of cooking.

See also:
Maple syrup glaze and Chinese spiced glaze,
Maple-glazed Pork Spare Ribs page 67

Tom-Tom Maple Syrup Glaze

This is especially good with pork and beef. You could use a 200 g (7 oz) can of chopped tomatoes instead of fresh tomatoes if you prefer.

1 small onion, chopped
2 garlic cloves, crushed
1 tablespoon olive oil
225 g (8 oz) ripe plum tomatoes, skinned, seeded and chopped
salt and freshly ground black pepper
1 sprig of fresh thyme
1 bay leaf
50 ml (2 fl oz) maple syrup
1 tablespoon sundried tomato paste
1 tablespoon dark soy sauce
salt and freshly ground black pepper

Fry the onion and the garlic in the oil for 5 minutes until soft.
Add the tomatoes, salt, pepper and herbs and simmer vigorously for 5 minutes until very well reduced and thick.
Remove the herbs from the sauce, spoon it into a food processor and blend until smooth. Stir in the maple syrup, sundried tomato paste, soy sauce and seasoning and start to brush on to the meat half way through cooking.

SAUCES

Ainsley's Sweet Chilli Sauce

This sauce is not as hot as one would expect, despite the amount of chillies. Used sparingly, it is a very refreshing accompaniment to almost any cooked meats and would go really well with anything from the Far East, and makes a great alternative dipping sauce for the Orla's Bamboo Thai Prawn Satay with Griddled Limes on page 47, the Million Meaty Satay Sticks on page 43 or the Krungthep Crab and Coconut Cakes on page 96. So many uses for one delightful easy-to-make sauce.

Makes 175 ml (6 fl oz)
150 g (5 oz) caster sugar
300 ml (10 fl oz) water
1 lime
100 g (4 oz) red finger chillies, trimmed, seeded and very finely chopped
6 fresh mint leaves, finely chopped

Put the sugar and water into a pan and leave over a low heat until the sugar has completely dissolved.
Meanwhile, remove the zest of the lime with a potato peeler, taking care not to remove the bitter white pith from underneath. Cut it into very fine shreds, bunch them together and very finely chop. Squeeze out the juice from the lime.
Bring the mixture to the boil, add the lime zest and cook for about 3 minutes until the syrup lightly coats the back of a spoon.
Add the chillies, remove from the heat and leave to cool before stirring in the mint.

My Classic Barbecue Sauce

Bottled sauces and ketchups are always great with any grilled meats but home-made ones are even better. This one will nicely jazz up and 'wash down' almost any burger or plainly barbecued meat.

Makes 450 ml (15 fl oz)
2 tablespoons sunflower oil
1 onion, finely chopped
2 garlic cloves, crushed
200 g (7 oz) can chopped tomatoes
2 tablespoons tomato purée
1 tablespoon light soft brown sugar
1 tablespoon Worcestershire sauce
a few drops of tabasco sauce
2 tablespoons white wine vinegar
1 tablespoon English mustard
salt and freshly ground black pepper

Heat the oil in a medium-sized pan. Add the onion and the garlic and fry over a medium heat for 7–8 minutes, stirring now and then, until the onions are soft and lightly browned.
Add the remaining ingredients to the pan and leave the sauce to simmer very gently for 10 minutes, giving it a stir every now and then, until it has slightly thickened.
If you want a smoother sauce, tip the mixture in a food processor and blend it for a few seconds. Serve hot or cold.

Soaking up the rays...
It ain't half hot, mum!
Outback, Australia.

Sweet and Sour Apricot Sauce

This rich and dark, slightly tangy-tasting sauce is great with any barbecued meats, especially pork.

Makes 450 ml (15 fl oz)
2 tablespoons sunflower oil
1 onion, very finely chopped
1 clove garlic, crushed
5 cm (2 in) fresh root ginger, peeled and
  finely grated
397 g (14 oz) can apricots in natural juice
3 tablespoons lemon juice
5 tablespoons light soft brown sugar
3 tablespoons dark soy sauce
75 ml (3 fl oz) white wine vinegar
2 tablespoons tomato purée
salt and freshly ground black pepper

Heat the oil in a medium-sized pan. Add the onion and fry for 5 minutes until soft and very lightly browned. Add the garlic and the ginger to the pan and fry for 1 minute.
Drain the canned apricots, reserving the juice. Put the apricots, 2 tablespoons of the juice and the lemon juice into a food processor and blend until smooth.
Add the apricot purée to the onions with the rest of the ingredients and leave the sauce to simmer for 25–30 minutes until reduced and thickened. Serve hot or cold.

Chiang-Mai Thai Dipping Sauce

These light, sweet and sour sauces are very popular all over the Far East and they are ideal for serving with plainly barbecued meats and fish. They are supposed to be quite spicy, but you can remove the seeds from the chillies before you slice them if you wish.

Makes 150 ml (5 fl oz)
6 tablespoons rice or white wine vinegar
4 tablespoons caster sugar
½ teaspoon salt
1 clove garlic, very finely chopped
2 red birdseye chillies, thinly sliced
1 teaspoon chopped fresh coriander
1 spring onion, trimmed and very thinly sliced

Mix together the vinegar and the sugar until the sugar has completely dissolved.
Now stir in the remaining ingredients and serve in little bowls as a dipping sauce or drizzled over simply grilled meats and fish.

Speckled Spicy Peanut Sauce

This sauce is the classic accompaniment to the Million Meaty Satay Sticks on page 43 but it would also go very well with any plain grilled meats, especially, chicken, lamb and beef. It can also be made into a more liquid dressing with a little more coconut milk for any crunchy vegetable salad.

Makes 250 ml (8 fl oz)

50 g (2 oz) roasted salted peanuts
2 tablespoons groundnut or sunflower oil
3 shallots, very thinly sliced
2 garlic cloves, very finely chopped
3 red birdseye chillies, seeded and very finely chopped
50 g (2 oz) crunchy peanut butter
175 ml (6 fl oz) canned coconut milk
75 ml (3 fl oz) water
1 tablespoon palm or dark muscovado sugar
2 tablespoons lime juice
1 teaspoon sambal oelek or chilli sauce (optional, for those who like things extra spicy)
1 teaspoon Thai fish sauce
salt and cayenne pepper

Coarsely grind the roasted peanuts in a coffee grinder or mortar and pestle.
Heat the oil in a small pan, add the shallots and fry until richly golden. Lift out of the oil with a slotted spoon and set aside.
Add the garlic and chillies to the pan and fry until softened.
Add the ground peanuts, peanut butter, coconut milk, water and sugar and simmer gently for 4–5 minutes until slightly thickened.
Stir in the fried onions, lime juice, sambal oelek, Thai fish sauce and season to taste with a little salt and cayenne pepper. Pour into a small serving bowl and serve warm.

Mellow Minty Yoghurt Sauce

This refreshing no-need-to-cook sauce goes really well with any barbecued lamb or chicken and is a classic accompaniment to any Indian or Middle Eastern meat dishes.

Serves 4

175 g (6 oz) Greek or wholemilk natural yoghurt
3 tablespoons chopped fresh mint
1 teaspoon mint jelly, warmed
salt and freshly ground black pepper

Simply mix all the ingredients together and chill for at least 1 hour before serving.

Best Ever Mustard French Dressing

This is really useful for tossing through salad leaves, stirring into hot potatoes and adding extra flavour to other salad-like side dishes.

Serves 8

2 tablespoons white wine vinegar
2 tablespoons Dijon mustard
8 tablespoons olive oil
salt and freshly ground black pepper

Mix the vinegar and mustard together in a small bowl.
Gradually whisk in the oil until thick and creamy. Season with salt and pepper and chill until required.

See also:

Sally's Salmon Steaks with Fresh Basil Sauce page 100
Maddie's Bacon, Sage and Monkfish Wrap with Aioli page 106

SAVOURY BUTTERS

For a simple barbecue treat, what could be better, as all these butters can be made in advance and will keep for up to 1 week in the fridge or up to 2 months in the freezer. They are wonderful cut into thin slices and served on top of any simply barbecued meats or vegetables, especially sweetcorn and baked potatoes. So... roll out the butter.

Each of these butters will be enough to serve about 8 people

Betty Blue Cheese Butter

Full of tempting flavours ready to ooze into succulent barbecued pork or chicken.

50 g (2 oz) slightly salted butter, softened
50 g (2 oz) blue cheese such as Roquefort, Stilton
  or Danish blue
25 g (1 oz) full-fat soft cream cheese
1 tablespoon chopped fresh parsley
salt and freshly ground black pepper

Whizz the butter, blue cheese and cream cheese in a food processor until smooth. Stir in the parsley and seasoning, shape into a roll and chill until firm or until required.

Sundried Tomato and Black Olive Butter

Adds colour and flavour to your barbecued chicken and steaks.

100 g (4 oz) slightly salted butter, softened
4 sundried tomatoes, very finely chopped
1 small clove garlic, crushed
1 tablespoon snipped fresh chives
25 g (1 oz) pitted black olives, drained and finely
  chopped
¼ teaspoon salt
freshly ground black pepper

Mix the butter with the rest of the ingredients. Spoon on to a sheet of clingfilm or non-stick baking parchment, shape into a roll and wrap up tightly. Chill until firm or until required.

Italian Pesto Butter

This will get you sucking your teeth, it's great! Try it with barbied chicken, lamb and white fish.

100 g (4 oz) slightly salted butter, softened
2 tablespoons pesto
2 heaped tablespoons chopped fresh basil
2 tablespoons finely grated Parmesan
1 clove garlic, crushed
salt and freshly ground black pepper

Mix the butter with the rest of the ingredients. Spoon on to a sheet of clingfilm or non stick baking parchment, shape into a roll and wrap up tightly. Chill until firm or until required.

Shallot, Mustard and Black Peppercorn Butter

This is superb with any grilled meats, especially steaks.

1 teaspoon sunflower oil
3 shallots, very finely chopped
100 g (4 oz) slightly salted butter, softened
1 tablespoon black peppercorns, coarsely crushed
1 teaspoon Dijon mustard
¼ teaspoon salt

Heat the oil in a small pan, add the shallots and fry gently for 6–8 minutes until golden brown.
Leave to cool and then beat into the butter with the peppercorns, mustard and salt.
Spoon on to a sheet of clingfilm or non-stick baking parchment, shape into a roll about 4 cm (1½ in) thick and wrap up tightly. Chill until firm or until required.

Five-spice, Orange and Ginger Butter

This goes very well with grilled pork or chicken.

100 g (4 oz) slightly salted butter
2.5 cm (1 in) fresh root ginger, peeled and very
  finely grated
finely grated rind of 2 small oranges
1 clove garlic, crushed
1 tablespoon freshly squeezed orange juice
1 teaspoon five-spice powder
¼ teaspoon salt
freshly ground black pepper

Mix the butter with the rest of the ingredients.
Spoon on to a sheet of clingfilm or non-stick
baking parchment, shape into a roll and wrap up
tightly. Chill until firm or until required.

See also:

Lemon and thyme butter, Spatchcocked Lemon
Poussins page 62
Caper, garlic and parsley butter, Chilli and orange
Butter and Tarragon, shallot and white wine butter,
Barbecued Lobster with Three-Flavoured Butters
page 94
Chilli and lime butter, Chargrilled Sweet Potatoes,
Pumpkin and Parsnips page 135

SALSAS

This is the Spanish word meaning sauce. These
are not the smooth, runny sauces we are familiar
with, but rather a piquant mixture of finely chopped
vegetables, herbs and sometimes fruit which are
very popular in Latin America, especially Mexico.
They make a wonderfully refreshing
accompaniment to all types of barbecued fish and
meats.

All these salsas will serve 6–8 people.

OPPOSITE Roasted Sweetcorn, Red Pepper and Avocado
Salsa and Sundried Tomato and Black Olive Butter
(see page 31)

Roasted Sweetcorn, Red Pepper and Avocado Salsa

This salsa needs to be finished with the avocado
just before serving because avocado soon
discolours once it has been chopped. I often eat
this on its own with barbecued ciabatta bread
slices, it's so good.

2 ears sweetcorn, husks removed
1 large red pepper
sunflower or vegetable oil for grilling
1 lemon
2 red chillies, seeded and very finely chopped
1 small red onion, very finely chopped
2 small, ripe but firm avocados
salt and freshly ground black pepper

Brush the ears of sweetcorn and the red pepper
with a little oil and barbecue or grill, turning now
and then. The peppers will take about 10 minutes
and the sweetcorn about 15, by which time they
should both be tender and slightly blackened in
places.
Drop the pepper into a plastic bag and seal. Leave
to cool together with the sweetcorn.
Stand the sweetcorn upright in a large mixing bowl
and drag the kernels off the cob with a fork.
Alternatively, slice them away from the cob with a
large knife.
Cut the grilled pepper in half and scoop out the
seeds. Turn it over and scrape away the skin with
a small sharp knife. Finely dice the flesh.
Thinly peel the zest off the lemon with a potato
peeler, leaving behind the bitter white pith. Very
finely chop the zest and then squeeze out the
lemon juice.
Mix the sweetcorn, pepper and lemon zest with
the red chilli, onion and 2 tablespoons of lemon
juice.This mixture can now be covered and set
aside in the fridge for 1 hour or until you are ready
to serve.
Halve the avocados and remove the stones. Scoop
out the flesh in as large pieces as possible and
cut it into small dice about the same size as the
sweetcorn kernels. Scrape out the avocado shells
and set to one side.
Stir the avocado and some salt and pepper into
the rest of the salsa.
Spoon the mixture back into the avocado shells
and serve straight away.

Mexican Aztec Tomato Salsa

The classic salsa, also called 'Salsa Ranchera', always found on the table in any home or restaurant. They say the contents change as easily as the funds of an embezzled bank. But it's still delicious.

6 tomatoes, skinned, seeded and diced
1 medium red onion, finely chopped
2 cloves garlic, crushed
2 tablespoons freshly squeezed lime juice
2 green chillies, seeded and very finely chopped
4 tablespoons chopped fresh coriander
salt and freshly ground black pepper

Mix all the ingredients together, spoon into a bowl and chill in the fridge for 1 hour.

Italian Tomato Salsa

All the flavours of the Mediterranean are captured here for your delight.

6 ripe plum tomatoes, skinned and seeded
1 small bunch of fresh basil
25 g (1 oz) pitted black olives, thinly sliced
3 shallots, thinly sliced
2 garlic cloves, very finely chopped
1 tablespoon extra virgin olive oil
2–3 teaspoons balsamic vinegar
salt and freshly ground black pepper

Cut the tomatoes into thin strips.
Discard the stalks from the basil, stack the leaves one on top of the other and very finely shred.
Gently mix together the tomatoes, basil, olives, shallots, garlic, olive oil, balsamic vinegar and some salt and pepper to taste. Spoon into a small bowl and serve straight away.

Cucumber and Caper Salsa

It's refreshingly cool with a tangy twist. This is made using similar ingredients to the classic Italian sauce, Salsa Verde, and is the perfect accompaniment to all types of barbecued fish.

½ cucumber
1 tablespoon capers, drained and rinsed
2 garlic cloves, very finely chopped
8 cocktail gherkins, very finely chopped
1 large sweet white onion or red onion, very finely chopped
3 tablespoons roughly chopped fresh flatleaf parsley
1 tablespoon chopped fresh mint
1 tablespoon lemon juice
1 tablespoon extra virgin olive oil
salt and freshly ground black pepper

Halve the cucumber lengthways and scoop out the seeds.
Cut the flesh into small dice and mix in a small bowl with the remaining ingredients. Chill for 1 hour before serving.

Mango and Pineapple Salsa

With its totally tropical taste, come rain or shine you'll always be smiling whilst munching this salad.

1 baby pineapple or 200 g (7 oz) canned pineapple in natural juice
1 small, ripe but firm mango
5 spring onions, trimmed and thinly sliced
1 red finger chilli, seeded and very finely chopped
2.5 cm (1 in) fresh root ginger, peeled and finely grated
3 tablespoons lime juice
1 tablespoon chopped fresh mint
salt and freshly ground black pepper

If you're using a fresh pineapple, slice off the top and the bottom, place it cut-side down on a board, slice away the skin and all the little brown 'eyes'.
Cut the fruit into quarters, remove the core and cut the flesh into small dice. Simply drain and chop the canned pineapple if using.
Peel the mango, slice the flesh away from either side of the flat stone and cut it into small dice.
Mix the pineapple and mango in a bowl with the spring onions, red chilli, grated ginger, lime juice, chopped mint and some salt and pepper to taste. Chill for 1 hour before serving.

CHUTNEYS AND RELISHES

The smoky flavour of barbecued foods can be transformed into something spectacular if you serve it with one of these delicious side dishes.

Cucumber and Ginger Sambal

This Thai relish is quite spicy, so if you don't like things too hot, cut down on the number of dried chillies. Because cucumbers always leach out water once they come into contact with anything salty, this is best made and eaten the same day.

Serves 6–8

2 cucumbers
1 onion, thinly sliced
1 red chilli, seeded and thinly sliced
2 tablespoons salt
6 small dried chillies
3 garlic cloves, very finely chopped
6 shallots, finely chopped
2.5 cm (1 in) galangal or fresh root ginger, peeled and chopped
100 g (4 oz) roasted salted cashew nuts or peanuts
3 tablespoons groundnut or sunflower oil
1 teaspoon black mustard seeds
¼ teaspoon ground turmeric
3 tablespoons caster sugar
175 ml (6 fl oz) white wine vinegar

Cut the cucumbers into very thin slices. Place in a colander with the onion and the sliced red chilli, mix in the salt and set aside to drain for 2 hours.
Rinse off the salt and allow the water to drain away. Spread the mixture out on lots of kitchen paper or clean tea towels and dry really well.
Soak the dried red chillies in hot water for 10 minutes until softened. Drain and put into a food processor together with the garlic, shallots, galangal or root ginger and 25 g (1 oz) of the cashew nuts. Blend the mixture to a coarse paste.
Heat the oil in a frying pan. Add the mustard seeds and as soon as they begin to pop, add the spice paste and turmeric and fry for 5 minutes, stirring now and then.
Add the sugar and vinegar and simmer for 5–7 minutes until the mixture has reduced and thickened. Leave to cool.
Coarsely chop the rest of the cashew nuts.
Transfer the cucumber mixture to a bowl and stir in the spice paste and the chopped nuts. Stir together well, spoon into a bowl and serve.

Summer Pickled Vegetables

Lightly cooked vegetables preserved in a little vinegar make a great partnership with any cooked meats. Make this at least a week in advance so the flavours can mature. If this amount is more than you need, don't worry. It can be kept in a cool dark place along with any other jams and chutneys for up to three months. You lucky people.

Serves 8–10

100 g (4 oz) cauliflower
100 g (4 oz) celery
100 g (4 oz) carrots
100 g (4 oz) cucumber
100 g (4 oz) red peppers
50 g (2 oz) French beans
50 g (2 oz) mangetout
50 g (2 oz) baby sweetcorn
50 g (2 oz) button onions
300 ml (10 fl oz) white wine vinegar
3 allspice berries
3 black peppercorns
4 fresh bay leaves
pinch of ground saffron or turmeric
2 garlic cloves, chopped
3 tablespoons light soft brown sugar
50 g (2 oz) cherry tomatoes
3 tablespoons olive oil
1 tablespoon chopped fresh dill
salt and freshly ground black pepper

Break the cauliflower into small florets.
Trim the celery and peel the carrots and cut them both diagonally into thickish slices.
Halve the cucumber, scoop out the seeds with a teaspoon and slice across into half-moons.
Halve the pepper, remove the seeds and cut the flesh into 1 cm (½ in) pieces.
Top and tail the beans, mangetout and sweetcorn and peel the button onions.
Put all the vegetables except the cherry tomatoes into a large pan with the vinegar, spices, garlic and sugar. Season with some salt and pepper, bring to the boil and simmer for just 5 minutes, carefully turning them over every now and then.
Transfer the mixture to a glass bowl, stir in the whole cherry tomatoes, olive oil and dill, cover and leave the mixture somewhere cool to marinate overnight.
The next day, spoon the vegetables into sterilized jars (see page 18) and seal. Store in a cool dark place for 1 week before eating. Store in the fridge once opened and eat within 1 week.

Beetroot Relish

This is a very unusual but very cooling yoghurt-style relish. There is no need to embark on the messy job of preparing fresh beetroot these days. You should find it already peeled and cooked on the salad counter of your local supermarket.

Serves 6–8

225 g (8 oz) cooked and peeled beetroot
½ teaspoon cumin seeds
2–3 teaspoons lemon juice
1 small onion, very finely chopped
½ tablespoon horseradish sauce (not creamed horseradish)
100 g (4 oz) wholemilk or Greek natural yoghurt
2 tablespoons chopped fresh mint
cayenne pepper and salt

Cut the beetroot into small dice and place in a bowl.
Heat a dry, heavy-based frying pan over a high heat. Add the cumin seeds and toss around for a couple of minutes until they start to smell aromatic and have darkened slightly.
Grind to a fine powder in a coffee grinder or a mortar and pestle.
Add the roasted cumin to the beetroot with the rest of the ingredients and stir together well. Cover and chill for 1 hour before serving.

Southern Sweetcorn Relish

You can make this tangy American-style relish some time in advance because it will keep, very much like jam, for two to three months in a cool, dark place. This is just the thing to make a beefburger heaven.

Serves 6–8

½ teaspoon salt
1 tablespoon plain flour
¼ teaspoon English mustard powder
a good pinch of ground turmeric
40 g (1½ oz) caster sugar
150 ml (5 fl oz) distilled malt vinegar
75 g (3 oz) white cabbage, cored and finely shredded
½ small onion, thinly sliced
1 small red pepper, seeded and chopped
1 small green pepper, seeded and chopped
275 g (10 oz) can sweetcorn, drained

Sift the salt, flour, mustard powder and turmeric together into a pan.
Stir in the sugar and vinegar and cook over a low heat for a few minutes until the sugar has dissolved.
Bring the mixture to the boil, add the cabbage and the onion and simmer for 10 minutes.
Stir in the red and green pepper and simmer for 15 minutes, stirring now and then.
Add the sweetcorn and simmer for 2 minutes. Spoon the mixture into sterilized jars (see page 18), seal and leave to cool.
This will keep in a cool, dark place for up to 3 months. Store in the fridge once opened and use within 1 week.

Speedy Tomato and Red Pepper Chutney

This chutney is very quick and easy to make and goes exceptionally well with any sausages, especially the Herby Home-made Sausagemeat Patties on page 91.

Serves 6–8

1 large onion, roughly chopped
1 large red pepper, seeded and chopped
15 g (½ oz) butter
1 tablespoon sunflower oil
½ teaspoon paprika
2 tablespoons demerara sugar
200 g (7 oz) can chopped tomatoes
1 tablespoon lemon juice
1 tablespoon Dijon mustard
1 tablespoon tomato purée
salt and freshly ground black pepper

Fry the onion and the red pepper in the butter and oil for 5 minutes until soft. Add the paprika and fry for 1 minute.
Add 1 tablespoon of the sugar and cook for a further 5 minutes, stirring now and then until the mixture has lightly caramelized.
Stir in the remaining ingredients, season with salt and pepper and leave the mixture to simmer for 10 minutes. You can serve this hot or cold with any barbecued meats.

See also:
Red Onion Marmalade (page 90)

OPPOSITE Eating with the fishermen at Paternoster Beach. There's no language barrier when it comes to good food.

COOKING TIMES

This chart will give you an idea of how long it will take to cook most types of fish and meat on a barbecue. However these timings are only approximate because it will not only depend on the thickness of the food (a 2.5 cm (1 in) thick piece of steak will take approximately the same time to cook through, whether it weighs 225 g (8 oz) or 450 g (1 lb)), but also on the heat of each individual barbecue, the distance of the rack from the coals and the weather on a cold day things will take a little longer to cook.

For larger joints of meat, the easiest way of telling if it is done to your liking is to push a meat thermometer into the thickest part of the meat to register the internal temperature, so I have given these as well as an approximate time. As with all roasts, it is important to remove larger joints of meat from the barbecue on to a board, cover tightly with a piece of foil and leave it to rest for 5–10 minutes before carving (during which time the internal temperature will rise by approximately another 10°C/25°F). This allows the meat to relax and gives time for the juices, which have been bubbling up to the surface during cooking, to soak back down into the meat, making it more moist and tender.

All these timings are for foods cooked over a medium-hot barbecue using the direct method (see page 14) unless otherwise stated.

FISH
As a general rule, allow 10 minutes per 2.5 cm (1 in) thickness of fish. Be very careful not to overcook it as it will dry out very quickly and become tasteless.

200–225 g (7–8 oz) fish steaks (about 2.5 cm (1 in) thick)	4–5 minutes each side
75–100 g (3–4 oz) fish fillets	1½–3 minutes each side depending on the thickness
275–350 g (10–12 oz) whole fish	6–7 minutes each side
1.5 kg (3 lb) large whole fish	12–15 minutes each side, or until the internal temperature reaches 50°C/125°F
large, raw prawns	2–3 minutes each side

CHICKEN
All chicken must be well cooked but not dried out. As a general rule, white breast meat will take less time to cook than the darker meat such as the thighs and drumsticks.

175 g (6 oz) boneless chicken breasts	7–8 minutes each side
175 g (6 oz) boneless thighs	4–5 minutes each side
275–300 g (10–11 oz) breasts on the bone	25 minutes, turning regularly
225 g (8 oz) drumsticks and thighs on the bone	15–20 minutes, turning regularly
250 g (9 oz) chicken quarters	25–30 minutes, turning regularly
750 g (1½ lb) chicken halves	35–40 minutes, turning regularly
450 g (1 lb) whole poussins	40 minutes or until the internal temperature reaches 85°C/185°F
1.5 kg (3 lb) whole chickens, cooked over indirect heat (allow 15 minutes per 450 g (1 lb) plus 15 minutes)	1 hour or until the internal temperature reaches 85°C/185°F
large chicken wings	20–25 minutes, turning regularly
chicken kebabs	10 minutes, turning regularly

LAMB

All these timings are for medium rare lamb. Decrease the timings slightly if you like it really pink and increase it a little if you prefer your lamb well done.

2.5 cm (1 in) thick loin lamb chops	6–7 minutes each side
175 g (6 oz) lamb fillets	4–5 minutes each side
4 cm (1½ in) thick leg of lamb steaks	6–7 minutes each side
larger joints, cooked over indirect heat (allow 20 minutes per 450 g (1 lb))	1 hour 10 minutes for a 1.5 kg (3½ lb) leg of lamb or until the internal temperature is 60°C/140°F
lamb kebabs	10–15 minutes turning regularly

PORK

It is important that pork is well cooked but it is very easy to dry it out. These timings will give you well-done pork which is still juicy.

2–2.5 cm (¾–1 in) thick boneless steaks	7–8 minutes each side
2.5 cm (1 in) thick chump or loin chops	8–10 minutes each side
450 g (1 lb) pork fillets	25 minutes, turning regularly
larger joints, cooked over indirect heat (allow 25–30 minutes per 450 g (1 lb) plus 25 minutes)	1¼–1½ hours for a 900 g (2 lb) boned and rolled loin of pork or until the internal temperature is 75°C/170°F
pork kebabs	12–15 minutes, turning regularly

BEEF

With steaks, it is best to sear them on each side first and then continue to cook them to your liking.

2.5–4 cm (1–1½ in) thick rump or sirloin steaks	Rare: 3–4 minutes on each side
	Medium: 5–6 minutes on each side
	Well done: 7 minutes on each side
4–5 cm (1½–2 in) thick fillet steak medallions	Rare: 4–5 minutes on each side
	Medium: 7–8 minutes on each side
	Well done: 8–9 minutes on each side
larger joints, cooked over indirect heat (allow 18–20 minutes per 450 g (1 lb))	1 hour for a 1.25 kg (2¾ lb) rolled sirloin or until the internal temperature is 65°C/150°F
2.5–4 cm (1–1½ in) thick beefburgers	Rare: 3–4 minutes on each side
	Medium: 5 minutes on each side
	Well done: 6–7 minutes on each side
beef kebabs	5–10 minutes, turning regularly

SAUSAGES

8–10 minutes, turning now and then

THE TOUCH TEST

Another simple way of testing meat for readiness is to press it lightly with your finger.
Rare: The meat will give easily and no juices will appear on the surface.
Medium: The meat will still be slightly springy but a few juices will be starting to appear on the surface.
Well done: The meat will be very firm to the touch and the surface will be covered with juices.

Open wide! For prawn
and lime satay.
Hua Hin, Thailand.

APPETIZERS

Parker's Pear and Parma Ham Bruschetta

I cooked these in the middle of a fruit farm in Paarl, South Africa. Often the simplest recipes turn out to be the most spectacular and by the look of the crew's faces after tasting them, I knew I was on to an absolute winner.

Serves 4
2 large ripe pears
4 slices rustic white bread
about 1 tablespoon extra virgin olive oil
8 thin slices Parma ham
175 g (6 oz) Gorgonzola
100 g (4 oz) mixed green salad leaves
about 2 tablespoons Best Ever French Dressing
   (see page 30)
salt and freshly ground black pepper

Cut the pears into slices about 5 mm (¼ in) thick and then cut out the core from each piece.
Place the pears onto the rack of the barbecue over medium-hot coals and cook for 2–3 minutes, turning once until they are heated through and lightly charred. Remove and set to one side.
Place the bread onto the barbecue and toast for 1–2 minutes. Turn over, drizzle with a little of the oil and then arrange 2 slices of the Parma ham on each piece. Top with a couple of pieces of the pear and then crumble the Gorgonzola on top.
Toss the salad leaves with the French dressing and some seasoning.
Divide between 4 shallow dishes, top with a piece of bread and serve at once, preferably with lots of sunshine and a glass of bubbly. Hmmmmm.

Fire-Roasted Red Pepper Guacamole

Here's my version of that creamy Mexican avocado dip which makes a great summertime starter with some crunchy tortilla chips. I've added a roasted red pepper to the mixture but you can leave it out if you wish.

Serves 6–8
1 large red pepper
3 large ripe avocados
1 small onion, very finely chopped
1 tomato, skinned, seeded and diced
2 green chillies, seeded and very finely chopped
4–5 tablespoons chopped fresh coriander
juice of 1 lime
salt and cayenne pepper
tortilla chips to serve

Barbecue or grill the red pepper for about 20 minutes, turning now and then until the skin is really quite black. Drop it into a plastic bag, seal and leave to cool.
Remove the pepper from the bag, peel off the skin and discard the seeds. Very finely chop the flesh.
Cut the avocados in half, remove the stones and scoop the flesh into a bowl. Mash with the back of a fork into a smooth purée.
Stir in the roasted red pepper, onion, tomato, green chillies, coriander, lime juice and some salt and cayenne pepper to taste and serve with the tortilla chips.

TIP: Leave the stone in the dip to prevent it from discolouring.

Million Meaty Satay Sticks

The streets of Thailand, especially in Bangkok, are littered with stalls serving millions of satay made with chicken, pork, lamb or beef.

Satay can either be cut into cubes or strips, which are marinated and then threaded or woven on to soaked bamboo skewers. They never fail to impress and always go down a storm. These are traditionally served with the Speckled Spicy Peanut Sauce on page 30.

Serves 6

450 g (1 lb) chicken breast fillet, lamb fillet, pork fillet or lean steak
1 teaspoon cumin seeds
1 teaspoon coriander seeds
½ teaspoon fennel seeds
1 stalk of lemongrass
4 shallots, very finely chopped
2 cloves garlic, finely chopped
2 tablespoons light soy sauce
1 teaspoon ground turmeric
½ teaspoon salt
1 tablespoon palm or light muscovado sugar
½ teaspoon mild or medium curry powder
4 tablespoons canned coconut milk
1 quantity Speckled Spicy Peanut Sauce (see page 30) to serve

12 x 15 cm (6 in) bamboo skewers soaked in cold water for 30 minutes

Cut the meat into 2 cm (¾ in) cubes or long strips about 1 cm (½ in) wide.

Heat a dry, heavy-based frying pan over a high heat. Add the cumin and coriander seeds and shake over the heat for a couple of minutes until they start to smell aromatic and have darkened slightly.

Grind to a fine powder with the fennel seeds in a coffee grinder or mortar and pestle.

Remove the tough outer leaves from the lemongrass and roughly chop the tender core. Put into a food processor with the shallots, garlic and soy sauce and whizz to a smooth paste.

Scrape the mixture into a large bowl and stir in the ground spices, turmeric, salt and sugar. Stir in the meat, cover and set aside to marinate for 2 hours at room temperature or overnight in the fridge.

Thread the cubes or strips of meat on to the skewers. Mix the curry powder with the coconut milk.

Barbecue the satay sticks for about 7–8 minutes, turning and basting with the coconut milk mixture now and then, until they are lightly browned on the outside but still moist and juicy in the centre. Arrange on a large plate and serve with the peanut sauce.

Buffalo Chicken Wings with Blue Cheese Dip

Crispy chicken wings make a great pre-feast nibble and this is a tasty way of turning what is often thought of as an off-cut into something scrumptious. They are cooked until the skin is quite crisp and then tossed in a tangy tomato sauce and served with a creamy dip and crunchy sticks of celery. My children love them and because they're so cheap to buy it's a very affordable barbecue feast.

Serves 6

24 large chicken wings
1 onion, finely chopped
1 garlic clove, crushed
40 g (1½ oz) butter
1 tablespoon light soft brown sugar
2 teaspoons English mustard powder
2 teaspoons chilli powder
250 ml (8 fl oz) tomato ketchup
120 ml (4 fl oz) red wine vinegar
1 tablespoon Worcestershire sauce
2 celery hearts, cut into chunky sticks

For the blue cheese dip:

100 g (4 oz) Danish Blue
1 garlic clove, crushed
3 tablespoons mayonnaise
1 tablespoon lemon juice
2 tablespoons finely chopped onion
4 tablespoons soured cream
a little chopped fresh parsley to garnish

12 long, flat metal skewers

For the blue cheese dip, put the cheese, garlic, mayonnaise and lemon juice into a food processor and blend until smooth. Stir in the chopped onion and soured cream.

Spoon the mixture into a bowl, sprinkle with the chopped parsley and set aside in the fridge until needed.

For the sauce fry the onion and garlic in the butter for 5 minutes until soft. Add the rest of the sauce ingredients and simmer for 3 minutes until thickened. Keep warm.

Cut the tips off the chicken wings and then thread them on to pairs of parallel skewers, so that they rest across the two like the rungs of a ladder. This makes it easier to turn them during cooking.

Barbecue the wings over medium-hot coals for about 20–25 minutes, turning regularly, until golden.

Slide the wings off the skewers into the pot of sauce and toss together well. Lift them out on to a plate and serve with the dip and celery sticks.

Dream Stuffed Mild Anaheim Chillies

Believe it or not these chillies are actually not that much hotter than the average green pepper and they take on a lovely sweet flavour when they are cooked, much like a pepper would. These are stuffed with a soft goats' cheese but a harder goats' cheese or an ordinary Cheddar will be just as tasty. Just cut the harder cheese into sticks about 10 cm (4 in) long and 1 cm (½ in) thick, ready for stuffing. When the locals tasted these chillies in Jamaica they said, 'Boy, dem chilli, dem taste wicked'.

Serves 4
8 large anaheim chillies
100–175 g (4–6 oz) soft goats' cheese
½ tablespoon olive oil
salt and freshly ground black pepper

Barbecue the chillies over medium-hot coals for 10–15 minutes, turning now and then, until the skin has blistered and charred and the flesh is just soft. Remove and leave to cool slightly and then carefully scrape off the skin with a small, sharp knife.
Make a cut lengthways down one side of each chilli and scoop out the seeds and the membranes with a teaspoon.
Spread a couple of tablespoons of the cheese into the centre of each one and then push them back into shape.
Brush the outside of the chillies with a little more oil, season well with salt and pepper and return them to the barbecue. Cook them for a few more minutes on each side until they are heated through and the cheese has melted. Serve straight away with perhaps some fresh crusty bread.

Mamma Tahsia's Baked Greek Olives

I first ate these when I visited a Greek friend's house, and that delicious taste has remained with me forever. Olives marinated in olive oil along with some other flavourings is nothing new, but this idea of serving them slightly warm is a little different and very tasty. All you have to do is ask Mamma Tahsia.

Serves 4
100 g (4 oz) pitted black, Greek Calamata olives
100 g (4 oz) pitted green olives
1½ tablespoons crushed coriander seeds
2 strips pared lemon zest, halved
2 strips pared orange zest, halved
2 small bay leaves, halved
2 cloves garlic, sliced
the leaves from 2 sprigs of fresh thyme
175 ml (6 fl oz) olive oil
2 tablespoons lemon juice
2 tablespoons orange juice
salt and freshly ground black pepper

Mix all the ingredients together in a bowl and set aside to marinate for at least 2 hours.
Shape 4 x 30 cm (12 in) squares of foil into little bowls and divide the olive mixture between them, making sure that each one gets a strip of lemon and lime zest and half a bay leaf.
Pinch the edges together to make well-sealed parcels and place to the side of the barbecue for 5 minutes until heated through. Remove, leave to cool slightly and serve with plenty of fresh crusty bread and wash down with chillied spicy white wine.

Orla's Bamboo Thai Prawn Satay with Griddled Limes

These are so easy to prepare yet so colourful and visually appetizing. The local Thai fishermen were so impressed that they wanted me to share some of the local 'Hard Stuff'. Needless to say, that was the end of the day's filming.

Serves 4

450 g (1 lb) raw, headless tiger prawns
1 stalk of lemongrass
3 limes
2 cloves garlic, finely chopped
120 ml (4 fl oz) canned coconut milk
6 tablespoons light soy sauce
2 teaspoons palm or light muscovado sugar

For the dipping sauce:

1 baby cucumber or a 5 cm (2 in) piece of ordinary cucumber
50 ml (2 fl oz) rice wine or white wine vinegar
1 tablespoon caster sugar
1 red birdseye chilli, seeded and finely chopped
2 teaspoons chopped roasted peanuts

8 x 15 cm (6 in) bamboo skewers soaked in cold water for 30 minutes

Peel the prawns if necessary, leaving the last tail segment in place.

Remove the tough outer leaves from the stalk of lemongrass and finely chop the tender core. Finely grate the zest from one of the limes and squeeze out the juice. Cut the remaining limes into small wedges.

Put the lemongrass, lime zest, lime juice, garlic, coconut milk, soy sauce and sugar into a non-metallic dish. Add the prawns, mix together well and set aside to marinate at room temperature for about 15 minutes or for up to 2 hours in the fridge.

For the dipping sauce, cut the cucumber in half and scoop out the seeds with a teaspoon. Cut the remaining cucumber into very small dice. Mix with the vinegar, sugar and chilli until the sugar has dissolved and then spoon into small serving bowls. Sprinkle over the peanuts.

Thread 4 prawns on to each skewer in pairs together with 2 lime wedges. Pierce through the tail of one prawn, add a lime wedge and then skewer the head end of the prawn so that it wraps itself around the lime attractively. Do this once more and repeat for the rest of the skewers.

Barbecue the skewers over a medium-hot coals for about 1 minute on each side or until just cooked through. Serve at once with the dipping sauce, garnished with the remaining lime wedges.

Melintzanosalata with Cherry Tomato Sticks

Almost every Greek cook has his or her version of this delicious aubergine dip and this is my one. (Not that I'm exactly Greek! But I do have many Greek friends.) You could make the whole thing in a food processor if you wish but I prefer the coarser texture that you achieve with a pestle and mortar. If you don't want to go to the trouble of making the tomato sticks to serve with the dip, serve as an accompaniment a range of crudités including radishes, cauliflower florets, carrot and cucumber batons and toasted pitta bread cut into fingers.

Serves 6
1 large aubergine
juice of ½ lemon
3–4 tablespoons extra virgin olive oil
good pinch of ground cumin
1 clove garlic, crushed
1 tablespoon chopped fresh flatleaf parsley
2 tablespoons Greek strained natural yoghurt
salt and freshly ground black pepper
For the tomato sticks:
450 g (1 lb) cherry tomatoes
4 cloves garlic, thinly sliced
24 small bay leaves
4 tablespoons olive oil

12 x 15 cm (6 in) bamboo skewers soaked in cold
   water for 30 minutes

Pierce the aubergines near the stem end with a fork – this will prevent them from popping during cooking.

Place them on to a medium-hot barbecue and cook for 20 minutes, turning now and then until the skin is really black and starting to blister and the flesh feels tender in the centre.

Meanwhile, for the cherry tomato sticks, thread 3 tomatoes on to the skewers, alternating them with a slice of the garlic and a bay leaf.

Cut the aubergines in half lengthways and scoop out the flesh into a pestle and mortar. Mash to a rough purée, then mix in the lemon juice.

Very gradually whisk in the olive oil as if you were making mayonnaise – the mixture will thicken very slightly. Stir in the ground cumin, garlic, parsley, yoghurt and seasoning to taste. Spoon into one or more bowls and drizzle with a little olive oil just before serving.

Brush the cherry tomato sticks with the olive oil and barbecue them over medium-hot coals for 4–5 minutes, turning every now and then, until they are just soft and the skins have split. Season with a little salt and pepper and serve together with the dip and the Garlic Pitta Fingers on page 150.

OPPOSITE Melintzanosalata with Cherry Tomato Sticks and Garlic Pitta Fingers (see page 150)

Spicy Mean Bean Dip with Plantain Chips

Cooked beans are a very popular ingredient in Jamaica and here I have turned them into an unusual dip to be served with some crunchy plantain chips. Plantains belong to the same family as the banana but they must be cooked before they can be eaten. They are sold at various stages of ripeness and for these chips you need to use the green, unripe ones. You can either cook them on the barbecue or deep-fry them.

Serves 6
397 g (14 oz) can red kidney or pinto beans
100 g (4 oz) soft cream cheese or goats' cheese
4 tablespoons soured cream
1 small red onion, very finely chopped
1 garlic clove, crushed
2 tomatoes, skinned, seeded and diced
2 red finger chillies, seeded and very finely chopped OR 2 teaspoons
    minced red chilli from a jar
2 tablespoons chopped fresh coriander
1 teaspoon lemon or lime juice
salt and freshly ground black pepper
For the plantain chips:
2 large green plantains
sunflower oil
sea salt to taste

For the dip, tip the beans into a sieve and rinse off the starchy liquid. Drain them really well, tip them into a bowl and crush into a rough paste with a potato masher.
Mix in the rest of the ingredients, spoon the dip into a bowl, cover and chill until you are ready to serve.
For the plantain chips, score the skin of the plantain and peel away the skin. Slice the fruit thinly on the diagonal into a bowl and stir in a little sunflower oil and a little salt. Toss them around a bit with your hands so that all the slices get well coated in the oil.
To cook the chips on the barbecue, lay them side by side on a fine-meshed rack (see page 16) and cook in batches for about 10 minutes on each side, brushing with a little more oil now and then, until they are crisp and have turned a deep golden brown.
As each batch cooks, tip them into a bowl (using oven gloves to hold the mesh rack) and once they are cold, sprinkle them with a little more salt to serve alongside the spicy bean dip.
Alternatively, deep-fry the chips at 180°C/350°F until crisp and golden. Drain on kitchen paper before sprinkling with the salt or a little sugar if you like a touch of sweetness.

Yakitori Skewers

These are the simplest of chicken kebabs with a very Japanese flavour. Unfortunately it is still not very easy to get hold of traditional Japanese ingredients. This is an authentic recipe for the marinade but you can substitute very dry sherry for the sake and dry sherry mixed with 1 teaspoon of caster sugar for the mirin if you wish. I've always got useful tips and alternatives for you so there's no excuse. Go on, have a go, you'll love 'em.

Serves 6–8
350 g (12 oz) chicken breast fillets
4 tablespoons Japanese soy sauce
2 tablespoons mirin
4 teaspoons sake
2 teaspoons caster sugar
4 shiitake mushrooms
4 spring onions, trimmed

16 x 15 cm (6 in) bamboo skewers soaked in cold water for
   30 minutes

Cut the chicken into 2 cm (¾ in) pieces.
Put the soy sauce, mirin, sake and sugar into a small pan. Bring to the boil and simmer for a few minutes until it has reduced a little and become slightly syrupy.
Remove the stalks from the mushrooms and cut each cap into quarters.
Cut each spring onion into 4 x 2.5 cm (1 in) pieces.
Thread 3 pieces of chicken onto each skewer, alternating them with a piece of mushroom and a piece of spring onion.
Brush the skewers generously with the marinade and barbecue over medium-hot coals for about 7 minutes, turning and basting with the leftover marinade now and then. A bottle or two of ice-cold Japanese lager is the perfect accompaniment.

Jerking chicken at
Strawberry Hill.
Blue Mountains,
Jamaica.

MAIN
COURSES

POULTRY

Jamaican 'Roast It, Don't Poke It' Chicken

This recipe can be used for large poussins, guinea fowl or small chickens, especially the corn-fed ones. You will just need to adjust the cooking times, allowing about 15 minutes per 450 g (1 lb) plus 15 minutes. You must have a covered barbecue for this recipe.

Serves 4
1 x 1.5 kg (3 lb) corn-fed chicken
1 teaspoon paprika
1 tablespoon mild curry powder
pinch of ground cloves
pinch of ground cinnamon
finely grated zest of ½ lemon
1 clove garlic, crushed
1 tablespoon chopped fresh coriander
¼ teaspoon salt
freshly ground black pepper
50 g (2 oz) butter, softened
2 fresh bay leaves

Remove the elastic from the legs and any giblets and excess fat from the chicken cavities.
Mix the paprika, curry powder, ground cloves, ground cinnamon, lemon zest, garlic, chopped coriander, salt and black pepper with the butter to make a smooth paste.
Loosen the skin over the breast of the chicken and spread about half of the curry butter over the breast meat in a thin layer.
Spread the rest of the butter inside the cavity of the chicken and then push in the bay leaves. Tie the legs back together with string and leave to stand for at least 1 hour.
Prepare your barbecue for the indirect method of cooking (see page 14).
Place the chicken directly over the tray, cover with the lid and cook for about 1 hour or until the juices run clear when the thickest part of the thigh is pierced with a thin metal skewer. Delicious with Peppy's Jamaican Rice and Peas on page 144. And for real authenticity a reggae disc of Bob Marley and a glass of Rum Pu-Punch on page 174.

Fuzzyless Jerk Chicken

Everywhere you go in Jamaica you'll find jerking of some sort, whether it be pork, beef, fish or indeed chicken. Everyone's got their favourite recipe. In Boston Bay, Fuzzy, a jerk specialist added over twenty different ingredients to his jerk pork. Wow! But somehow I think life's too short, so check out my recipe. Habaneros or scotch bonnet chillies are the hottest chillies in the world, so go easy. This recipe is quite hot but certainly not overpowering but you can adjust the amount of these chillies that you use, or just use a milder type of chilli – after a few goes, you'll soon find a happy medium.
Lick it back with a tall glass of iced Mango and Pineapple Cooler on page 170.

Serves 6
6 part-boned chicken breasts or 16 large chicken wings
For the jerked sauce:
225 g (8 oz) onions, quartered
2 habaneros or scotch bonnet chillies, halved and seeded
50 g (2 oz) fresh root ginger, peeled and roughly chopped
½ teaspoon ground allspice
the leaves from 15 g (½ oz) fresh thyme sprigs
1 teaspoon freshly ground black pepper
120 ml (4 fl oz) white wine vinegar
120 ml (4 fl oz) dark soy sauce

Put all the ingredients for the jerked sauce into a food processor and whizz until smooth.
Place the chicken in a large shallow dish, pour over the sauce, cover and leave to marinate in the fridge for 24 hours, turning the chicken every now and then.
Barbecue the chicken breasts over medium-hot coals for 25–30 minutes and the wings for 20–25 minutes, basting now and then with the leftover sauce. As it cooks the thick sauce will go quite black in places, but as it falls off it will leave behind a really well flavoured, crisp skin, with lovely moist tender meat underneath.
Need I say that Peppy's Jamaican Rice and Peas on page 144 goes exceptionally well with the chicken and, for extra crunch, how about Ainsley's Ultimate Creole Cabbage Salad on page 139.

Munchie Mustard Chicken Escalopes

The idea of this dish is to cover a chunk of toasted ciabatta with baby leaf salad (buy a bag of ready-prepared leaves if you wish), add a piece of the grilled chicken escalope and finish it off with a good dollop of mustard mayonnaise. Delicious! Happy munching.

Serves 4
4 large chicken breast fillets
4 tablespoons olive oil
2–3 tablespoons Dijon mustard
1 garlic clove, crushed
1 loaf of ciabatta
1 teaspoon lemon juice
snipped fresh chives to garnish
salt and freshly ground black pepper
For the salad:
50 g (2 oz) baby spinach leaves
1 bunch of watercress, large stalks removed
½ small radicchio lettuce
4 tablespoons mayonnaise
1 tablespoon Dijon mustard

Place the chicken breasts one at a time between 2 large sheets of clingfilm and beat out gently with a rolling pin until they are about 5 mm (¼ in) thick and have almost doubled in size.
Mix 3 tablespoons of the oil with the mustard and the crushed garlic. Brush some of this mixture over both sides of the chicken, season with salt and pepper and set to one side.

For the salad, place the prepared leaves into a bowl and lightly toss together. Mix the mayonnaise with the mustard and set aside with the salad.
Cut the ciabatta in half lengthways as if you were going to make a sandwich and then across into 4 chunky pieces. Place cut-side down on the barbecue and leave for a couple of minutes until lightly toasted. Remove and set aside.
Barbecue the chicken over medium-hot coals for about 3 minutes on each side until golden on the outside but still juicy in the centre.
Whisk the rest of the olive oil, lemon juice and some salt and pepper into the remaining mustard mixture. Add to the salad leaves and toss together lightly.
Place a piece of ciabatta on to each plate and spread with a little mustard mayonnaise. Sprinkle over a few leaves, then put the chicken on top, followed by more leaves. Add another dollop of the mustard mayonnaise and sprinkle with a few snipped chives. Serve the awaiting munchers.

OPPOSITE Munchie Mustard Chicken Escalopes

Balinese Chicken

For this recipe, a thick spice and coconut paste is spread under the skin of the chicken instead of over the outside. This helps it to flavour the meat and prevents the tasty paste from over-browning and dropping off into the fire during cooking. Go easy when lifting the skin off the chicken and remember fingers only. No knives or you'll pierce the skin!

Serves 6
6 part-boned chicken breasts
5 cm (2 in) galangal or fresh root ginger, peeled and chopped
2 garlic cloves, crushed
1 stalk lemongrass, roughly chopped
2 red birdseye chillies, seeded and chopped
2 teaspoons ground turmeric
2 tablespoons chopped fresh coriander
6 spring onions, trimmed and chopped
2 fresh kaffir lime leaves, finely shredded or the finely grated zest
   of 1 lime
75 g (3 oz) creamed coconut

6 fine metal trussing skewers or cocktail sticks soaked in cold water
   for 30 minutes

Put the galangal or root ginger, garlic, lemongrass, chillies, turmeric, coriander, spring onions, and lime leaves or lime zest into a food processor and blend to a coarse paste.
Melt the creamed coconut in a small pan, stir in the paste and leave to cool slightly until thickened but not set hard.
Loosen the skin of each breast with your fingers, leaving it attached along one long edge. Spread the paste over the breast meat, lift the skin back into place and secure the open edge with a skewer or cocktail stick.
Barbecue the chicken over medium-hot coals for 25 minutes, turning regularly, until the skin is crisp and golden. Remove the skewers or cocktail sticks before serving. Serve with the Cool Carrot, Cumin and Lemon Salad on page 144.

Chargrilled Pineapple Chicken Kiss-Kiss

Here is a very simple dish with a real taste of summer.

You will now find ready prepared pineapples on the fruit section of most supermarkets. However, using fresh means you can use the skin of your pineapple to sit your cooked chicken on and it'll look great. Simply top and tail the pineapple, stand it upright and cut it into 6–8 wedges. Lay it skin-side down on a board and cut between the skin and the flesh from top to bottom.

Serves 6

6 large boneless chicken breasts, unskinned
225 g (8 oz) prepared fresh pineapple or canned pineapple in
  natural juice
2–3 spring onions, trimmed and thinly sliced
3 tablespoons caster sugar
pinch of chilli powder
salt and freshly ground black pepper

6 fine metal trussing skewers or cocktail sticks, soaked in cold
  water for 30 minutes

Cut a small shallow pocket into the side of the thickest part of each chicken breast.
Drain the pineapple and reserve the juice.
Finely chop the pineapple and mix with the spring onions and a little salt and pepper. Spoon the mixture into each pocket and secure in place with a skewer or cocktail stick.
Mix the pineapple juice and sugar together in a small pan and leave over a low heat until the sugar has dissolved. Bring the mixture to the boil and boil vigorously until it is syrupy and reduced to about 4 tablespoons. Stir in the chilli powder.
Barbecue the chicken over medium-hot coals for about 10 minutes, turning now and then, until it's about half-cooked. Then brush over some of the pineapple glaze and continue to cook for another 10 minutes, turning and brushing the chicken with more glaze, until it is cooked through and the skin is nice and golden. Once you've tasted it, you'll discover that 'kiss-kiss' appeal.

Griddled Chicken and Bacon Rolls

This is a very simple barbecue dish which can be prepared well in advance. You can vary the fillings very easily and those pick-and-mix portions of cheese from the supermarket are just the right size for one chicken breast. Oooh, now that sounds nice!

Serves 6
6 chicken breast fillets
2 tablespoons tomato ketchup
6 Lincolnshire sausages, skinned
6 rashers rindless back bacon

6 fine metal trussing skewers or cocktail sticks soaked in cold water for 30 minutes

Place the chicken breasts one at a time between 2 large sheets of clingfilm and flatten very slightly with a rolling pin.
Spread the underside of each piece with the tomato ketchup and then lay one of the sausages across the fatter end of each one.
Fold the chicken around each sausage, wrap each one in a rasher of bacon and secure in place with a skewer or cocktail stick.
Barbecue over medium-hot coals for about 25 minutes, turning now and then, until golden. Remove the skewers or cocktail sticks before serving.

VARIATIONS
- Stuff the chicken with different flavoured sausages.
- Replace the tomato ketchup with mustard.
- Leave out the tomato ketchup and substitute the sausages for 25 g (1 oz) sticks of coarse pork pâté or cheese such as Cheddar, Gruyère or Danish Blue.
- Spread the chicken with pesto and stuff with a couple of basil leaves and a 25 g (1 oz) stick of Mozzarella.

LEFT Enjoying the peace and tranquility. Australia.
OPPOSITE Griddled Chicken and Bacon Rolls with Ainsley's Ultimate Creole Cabbage Salad (see page 139)

Spatchcocked Lemon Poussins

A whole chicken is quite difficult to cook on a barbecue unless you are using a kettle, because they tend to blacken on the outside too much before they are cooked through in the centre. So here I have used little poussins instead which, once opened out flat, will cook in about 40 minutes.

Serves 4
4 x 450 g (1 lb) poussins
2 small lemons, thinly sliced
salt and freshly ground black pepper
For the lemon and thyme butter:
50 g (2 oz) slightly salted butter, softened
finely grated zest of ½ small lemon
1 teaspoon fresh thyme leaves, roughly chopped

8 x 25 cm (10 in) flat metal skewers

To spatchcock the poussins, place them breast-side down on a chopping board. Cut down either side of the backbone with poultry shears or a sharp pair of kitchen scissors and lift it out.
Turn the poussins over, open them out and press down firmly along the breast bone until they lie flat.
Loosen the skin over the breast of each one with your fingers and push about 3 slices of lemon underneath so that they lie down the centre of the breast meat. Finally thread 2 skewers diagonally through the birds to help hold them flat during cooking. You can now set them aside until you are ready to cook.
Meanwhile, mix the butter with the lemon zest, thyme, ¼ teaspoon of salt and some pepper. Spoon the butter into the centre of a sheet of clingfilm or non-stick baking parchment, shape into a roll and chill in the fridge until firm or until required.
Barbecue the poussins, bone-side down, for 25 minutes until almost done. Then turn them over and cook for another 15 minutes until the skin is crisp and golden and they are cooked through. Season on both sides with a little salt and pepper.
Remove the butter from the fridge and cut it into thin slices. Place a couple of slices of butter on to the top of each poussin and cook for a further 2–3 minutes until the butter has melted. Serve with salad and a few bottles of ice-cold lager.

Ostrich and Vegetable Sosaties

This dish is regularly featured on Portia de Smidt's menu at her famous restaurant, 'The African Cafe', in Cape Town. She's a brilliant cook as you'll discover when you expose your tastebuds to this wonderful dish. These days ostrich is available in larger supermarkets but you can easily substitute it with chicken or lamb if you wish.

Serves 4
1 kg (2¼ lb) ostrich fillet
1 large red, green and yellow pepper
1 ear of sweetcorn
4 baby marrows or courgettes
4 mini patty pan squash
For the meat and vegetable marinades:
1 small bunch (25 g (1 oz)) of fresh coriander
2 teaspoons salt (or to taste)
300 ml (10 fl oz) olive oil
12 large garlic cloves
225 g (8 oz) apricot jam
2 teaspoons ground cumin
90 ml (2½ fl oz) South African Pinotage or other fruity red wine
150 ml (5 fl oz) lemon juice

8 x 25 cm (10 in) flat metal skewers

Put half the coriander for the marinade, salt, oil and garlic into a food processor with all the jam, cumin and red wine and blend until smooth.
Cut the ostrich fillet into 4 cm (1½ in) cubes. Place them into a non-metallic bowl and stir in the jam-flavoured marinade.
Place the remaining coriander, salt, oil and garlic into a clean food processor with the lemon juice and blend until smooth.
Halve all the peppers, remove the seeds and cut them into rough 2.5 cm (1 in) cubes. Cut the ear of sweetcorn across into 2.5 cm (1 in) thick slices. Cut the baby marrow or courgettes across into 2.5 cm (1 in) thick slices and cut the patty pan squash into similar sized pieces.
Place all the vegetables into another bowl and stir in the second marinade. Cover both bowls and leave to marinate in the fridge overnight.
The next day, thread the meat and the vegetables alternately on to the skewers and barbecue over medium-hot coals for 10–12 minutes, turning now and then and basting with the leftover meat marinade.

Coco-Chicken and Mango Skewers

The smell of these chicken skewers is sensational and the orange of the mango and green of the peas make these into attractive as well as tasty kebabs, flavoured with Thai green curry paste and coconut milk. I bet you're licking your lips.

Serves 4
450 g (1 lb) chicken breast fillets
1 large, ripe but firm mango
50 g (2 oz) mangetout (about 24)
For the marinade:
120 ml (4 fl oz) canned coconut milk
1 tablespoon Thai green curry paste
1 teaspoon prepared minced lemongrass
  from a jar
1 teaspoon palm or light muscovado sugar
1 tablespoon Thai fish sauce
1 tablespoon groundnut or sunflower oil
finely grated zest of ½ lime
1 teaspoon lime juice

8 x 25 cm (10 in) bamboo skewers soaked in cold
  water for 30 minutes.

Cut the chicken into 2.5cm (1 in) cubes.
Mix together all the marinade ingredients, stir in the chicken and leave it to marinate for 2 hours at room temperature or overnight in the fridge.
Peel the mangoes and then slice the flesh away from either side of the thin flat stone and cut it into 1 cm (½ in) pieces.
Drop the mangetout into a pan of boiling salted water. Bring them back to the boil, drain and refresh under running cold water.
Thread 3 pieces of chicken and 3 mangetout folded around 3 pieces of mango alternately on to each skewer.
Barbecue the skewers over medium-hot coals for 10 minutes, turning now and then and brushing with the leftover marinade, until the chicken is lightly browned. These would be nice served with the Nice Rice Noodle Doodle Salad on page 138.

ABOVE Exciting exotic ingredients … No wonder Thai food is so enticing.
OPPOSITE Coco-chicken and Mango Skewers with Nice Rice Noodle Doodle Salad (see page 138)

PORK

Fragrant Thai Pork 'Roast'

This dish needs to be cooked in a covered barbecue using the indirect method (see page 14). Ask a butcher to prepare the right cut of pork for you because you will not be able to find it in an ordinary supermarket. Ask him for a skinned and rolled loin of pork made up of just the 'eye' of the meat. This does away with most of the fat, leaving a lean joint which goes superbly with the Thai flavoured marinades. I know it's a little extravagant but boy, is it worth it!

Serves 6
900 g (2 lb) boned, skinned and rolled loin of pork
2 tablespoons sunflower oil
½ teaspoon prepared tamarind from a jar
1 teaspoon prepared minced lemongrass from a jar
120 ml (4 fl oz) water
75 ml (3 fl oz) canned coconut milk
½ tablespoon palm or light muscovado sugar
¼ teaspoon salt
For the dry marinade:
1 teaspoon chopped fresh coriander
1 teaspoon chopped fresh basil
1 teaspoon desiccated coconut
½ teaspoon ground turmeric
1 teaspoon hot chilli powder
1 tablespoon palm or light muscovado sugar
½ teaspoon salt
For the wet marinade:
1 green finger chilli, seeded and roughly chopped
2 garlic cloves
2 shallots or ½ small red onion
25 g (1 oz) ground almonds
25 g (1 oz) fresh root ginger, peeled and roughly chopped
1 fresh kaffir lime leaf or 1 strip pared lime zest, chopped

Mix the dry marinade ingredients together in a large bowl. Add the pork and give it a few turns so that it becomes well coated in the mixture. Cover and set aside at room temperature for 1 hour.
Meanwhile, put the wet marinade ingredients into a food processor and blend to a smooth paste.
Heat the oil in a frying pan. Add the spice paste, tamarind and lemongrass paste and fry for about 3 minutes until the mixture splits away from the oil. Add the water and simmer for 2 minutes.

Add the coconut milk, sugar and salt and simmer for a further 2 minutes. Taste the sauce and adjust the seasoning if necessary.
Prepare your barbecue for the indirect method of cooking (see page 14).
Pour the wet marinade over the pork and turn the pork once or twice until well coated. Place the pork directly over the drip tray, cover the barbecue with the lid and cook the pork for 1–1¼ hours, spooning over the remaining wet marinade now and then, until the juices run clear when the centre of the pork is pierced with a thin skewer.
Transfer the pork to a board, cover with a sheet of foil and leave the meat to relax for 5 minutes. Carve it into thin slices and serve.

Uncle's Pork Calypso

Boneless pork chops or steaks cooked in this spicy rum and sugar glaze take on a typically tropical taste which reminds me of when I was a young boy and we had summer parties in the garden. My uncles would walk through the front door, smell the cooking and call out 'Peppy (my Mum), the pork calypso smell sweeeet!'. Make sure that the chops or steaks are about 2.5 cm (1 in) thick so that they stay nice and juicy during cooking.

Serves 4
4 x 175 g (6 oz) boneless pork chops or steaks
2.5 cm (1 in) fresh root ginger, peeled and finely grated
2 garlic cloves, crushed
2 tablespoons dark muscovado sugar
2 tablespoons sunflower oil
a good pinch of allspice
2 tablespoons dark rum
2 tablespoons pineapple juice

Mix the ginger, garlic, sugar, oil, allspice, rum and pineapple juice together in a shallow dish.
Add the pork to the marinade, turn once or twice in the mixture, cover and leave to marinate at room temperature for 2 hours or overnight in the fridge.
Barbecue the chops over medium-hot coals for 6–7 minutes on each side, basting with the leftover marinade now and then. These would be nice served with Peppy's Jamaican Rice and Peas on page 144 or the Caribbean Mixed Bean and Cashew Nut Salad on page 139 plus some calypso music, several uncles and plenty of Rum Pu-Punch on page 174.

Maple-glazed Pork Spare Ribs

Unfortunately most supermarkets sell single ribs, but if you can get them in racks from a butcher it will make things much easier and quicker when you come to turn them over. Pre-cooking them in the oven or boiling them in water with a teaspoon of mixed herbs before glazing them on the barbecue ensures that they will be really nice and tender at the end.

Serves 4
2 kg (4 lb) meaty pork spare ribs in 2 or 3 racks if possible
150 ml (5 fl oz) maple syrup
¼ teaspoon cayenne pepper
½ teaspoon salt
½ teaspoon ground black pepper
2 garlic cloves, crushed
2 tablespoons tomato purée
1 tablespoon Dijon mustard
2 tablespoons lemon juice

Preheat the oven to 190°C/375°F/Gas mark 5. Lay the ribs in a large, foil-lined roasting tin and cook for 45 minutes until tender. The ribs can be set aside at this stage until you are ready to finish them on the barbecue if you wish.
Mix the remaining ingredients together in a bowl.
Brush the ribs with some of the glaze and barbecue over medium-hot coals for 10–15 minutes, turning them now and then and basting with more of the glaze, until they are tender and lightly browned.
Give them one last coating of glaze so that they are nice and sticky, remove them on to a board and cut between the bones into single ribs. Serve with plenty of napkins and finger bowls to hand but you'll be sucking those fingers regardless.

VARIATION
Chinese Glazed Ribs Mix 150 ml (5 fl oz) clear honey, 1 tablespoon five-spice powder, 1 teaspoon salt, 1 teaspoon ground sichuan pepper, 2 crushed garlic cloves, 2 tablespoons ginger juice (see page 18), 2 tablespoons Chinese plum sauce and 2 tablespoons dry sherry together and use in place of the maple glaze.

Chinese Lattice Pork

This dish a has a truly oriental flavour, because although I have called it 'Chinese' it is made using a ready-made Japanese teriyaki sauce. This would be great served with some plain steamed rice and maybe the Oriental Mixed Vegetable Parcels on page 126.

Serves 4
700 g (1½ lb) piece of belly pork once the skin and bones have been removed
2.5 cm (1 inch) fresh root ginger, peeled
75 ml (3 fl oz) bottled teriyaki marinade
1 tablespoon dark soy sauce
4 tablespoons clear honey
2 tablespoons chilli sauce
2 teaspoon sesame oil
1 garlic clove, crushed

Cut the belly pork into 4 pieces. Make shallow, diagonal cuts, no more than 3 mm (⅛ in) deep, across both sides of the meat.
Finely grate the ginger on to a plate and squeeze out the juice into a shallow non-metallic dish.
Stir in the rest of the marinade ingredients and then add the pork.
Turn it over a few times so that it is well coated in the marinade, cover and leave at room temperature for 2 hours or for up to 24 hours in the fridge, turning it every now and then.
Barbecue the pork over medium-hot coals for 6–8 minutes on each side, basting all the time with the leftover marinade, until it has taken on a rich, glossy brown colour on the outside but is still moist and juicy in the centre.

Cheesy Mush-stuffed Pork Chops

If you're one of those people who enjoy a good cheesy stuffing, you'll love these pork chops. Buy chops which are at least 2.5 cm (1 in) thick for this recipe so that you have enough meat in which to make a pocket for stuffing.

Serves 4
4 x 200 g (7 oz) thick loin pork chops
salt and freshly ground pepper
For the cheese and mushroom stuffing:
1 small onion, very finely chopped
1 tablespoon olive oil
100 g (4 oz) button or chestnut mushrooms, finely chopped
100 g (4 oz) Cheddar, finely grated
2 tablespoons chopped fresh sage

4 fine metal trussing skewers or cocktail sticks soaked in cold water for 30 minutes

Make a horizontal cut through the fatty side of each chop into the eye of the meat almost through to the bone. Open up the meat into a pocket with your fingers.
For the stuffing, fry the onion in the oil for 5 minutes until soft and lightly browned. Add the mushrooms and fry for another 3–4 minutes until all the juices have evaporated and you are left with a thick mixture. Scrape it into a bowl and leave to cool.
Stir the grated cheese, sage and some seasoning into the mushroom mixture.
Spoon some of the stuffing into the pocket of each chop and secure the edges with a skewer or cocktail stick.
Season the chops on both sides with salt and pepper and barbecue over medium-hot coals for 20 minutes, turning frequently, until the pork is cooked through and the cheese in the centre has melted. Yummy... now, get ready for lift off.

OPPOSITE Char Sui Lettuce Rolls

Char Sui Lettuce Rolls

Char sui is the Chinese name for that infamous 'red' roast pork dish which you can get in almost every Chinese restaurant. Here I have served it carved into very thin slices, rolled up inside lettuce leaves with crunchy spring onions and cucumber strips. You could either serve this up as a main course or it would make a lovely mid-course for about 6 people.

Serves 4
2 x 450 g (1 lb) pork fillets
5 cm (2 in) fresh root ginger, peeled
1 large garlic clove, crushed
2 tablespoons Hoisin sauce
2 tablespoons dark soy sauce
2 teaspoons light soft brown sugar
1 teaspoon five-spice powder
2 tablespoons sunflower oil
4–6 drops red food colouring (optional)
2 tablespoons clear honey
To serve:
½ cucumber
6 spring onions, trimmed
1 large iceberg lettuce, broken into leaves
12 tablespoons Chinese plum sauce

Trim any fat and membrane of the outside of the pork fillets.
Finely grate the ginger and squeeze out the juice into a shallow non-metallic dish. Stir in the rest of the marinade ingredients.
Add the pork fillets and turn them over in the mixture until they are really well coated. Cover and set aside for at least 2 hours.
Cut the cucumber in half lengthways and scoop out the seeds with a teaspoon. Cut into thin strips about 7.5 cm (3 in) long. Halve the spring onions and cut lengthways into very thin shreds. Arrange on a serving plate in separate piles along with the lettuce leaves and a small bowl of the plum sauce.
Barbecue the pork fillets over medium-hot coals for about 20 minutes, turning now and then and basting with the leftover marinade, until the juices run clear when the meat is pierced with a skewer.
Transfer the pork to a board, carve it into very thin slices and then pile it on to a warmed serving plate. Instruct everyone to take a lettuce leaf and place a line of cucumber strips, shredded spring onion and sliced pork down the centre. Then spoon over a little plum sauce, roll the lettuce leaf up into a parcel to eat!

LAMB

St Giorgios Kleftiko Parcels

The ancient Greek method of cooking in a sealed pit was supposed to have been developed by the Kleftes, a band of Greek guerrillas, who fought against the Turks during the nineteenth century, so that the smell of their cooking didn't give away their hideout. In this recipe the pit has been replaced with a foil parcel, but the principle of sealing in all the delicious flavours (and aromas) during cooking remains the same. Hence the neighbour won't know you're having a barbie? Good ole parcels. And for a change, why not try chicken (skinned and boned chicken thighs are great) instead of lamb?

Serves 4
750 g (1½ lb) boned leg of lamb, well trimmed
65 ml (2½ fl oz) extra virgin olive oil
juice of 1 lemon (about 3 tablespoons)
2 teaspoons roughly chopped fresh oregano
2 teaspoons picked fresh thyme leaves
4 garlic cloves, finely chopped
2 small beef tomatoes, skinned, seeded and chopped
175 g (6 oz) kefalotyri cheese or goat's cheddar or pecorino
4 small bay leaves
salt and freshly ground black pepper

Place the lamb in a large bowl and pour over the olive oil, then add the lemon juice, oregano, thyme, garlic and salt and pepper. Mix together well and leave to marinate at room temperature for 2 hours or in the fridge overnight.
Shape 4 x 30 cm (12 in) squares of double thickness foil into little bowls. Sprinkle the tomatoes over the lamb mixture and then divide it between the pieces of foil. Arrange slices of cheese on top and stick a bay leaf in each parcel.
Pinch the edges of the foil together to make well-sealed parcels and barbecue over low-medium coals for 30–40 minutes until the lamb is completely tender and the cheese has begun to melt. These would be nice served with the Garlic Pitta Fingers on page 150 and a crisp green salad. Retsina, anyone?

Colourful Calabrian Lamb Patties

Cooking this on the famous flat rock in Hunter Valley overlooking spectacular vineyard views will live with me forever. Great food, great views and great company. The perfect barbecue ingredients alright, and loads of sunshine too. It was F.A.B.

Serves 4
450 g (1 lb) lean minced lamb
2 tablespoons olive oil
1 small red onion, very finely chopped
1 garlic clove, crushed
50 g (2 oz) fresh baby spinach leaves
25 g (1 oz) sundried tomatoes in oil, drained and roughly chopped
25 g (1 oz) fresh white breadcrumbs
25 g (1 oz) pine kernels, lightly toasted
100 g (4 oz) Tomme de Chèvre, Fontina or Cheddar
2 tablespoons chopped fresh basil
salt and freshly ground black pepper

Heat the oil in a small pan. Add the onion and the garlic and cook for 5 minutes until soft.
Remove the stalks from the spinach and wash the leaves in cold water. Dry off well (a salad spinner would be ideal) and then bunch the leaves together and cut them into very fine shreds.
Stir the spinach into the onion mixture and cook for 1–2 minutes until it has just wilted. Spoon into a mixing bowl and leave until cold.
Add the rest of the ingredients to the bowl and mix together well.
Shape the mixture into about 12 small patties and cook them over medium-hot coals for 2–3 minutes on each side or until completely cooked through and tender.

Luscious Lamb and Apricot Kebabs

The sweetness of both the lamb and the apricots is complemented beautifully by the tangy flavour of this unusual sweet and sour sauce. It's not from China as you might expect, but actually South Africa. The presence of the milk in the marinade might sound a bit odd, but it helps make the lamb unbelievably tender.

Serves 6

1 kg (2¼ lb) boned leg of lamb
1 small garlic clove, peeled but left whole
3 fresh bay leaves, bruised
¼ teaspoon ground ginger
½ teaspoon ground coriander
50 ml (2 fl oz) milk
¼ teaspoon freshly ground black pepper
1 teaspoon salt
75 g (3 oz) dried apricots (not the no need-to-soak ones)
2 small onions

For the sauce:

6 dried apricots
25 g (1 oz) butter
2 large onions, finely chopped
1 small red finger chilli, seeded and very finely chopped
1 tablespoon medium curry powder
½ teaspoon ground turmeric
350 ml (12 fl oz) lamb or vegetable stock
4 tablespoons caster sugar
120 ml (4 fl oz) white wine vinegar
½ teaspoon salt
2 teaspoons cornflour

6 x 25 cm (10 in) metal skewers

The day before the barbecue, cut the clove of garlic in half and rub all over the inside of large mixing bowl.

Trim the excess fat and the skin off the lamb and cut it into 4 cm (1½ in) cubes. Place it into the bowl with the remaining pieces of garlic, the bay leaves, ginger, coriander, milk, black pepper and salt and mix together well. Cover and leave in the fridge to marinate overnight.

Place the 6 dried apricots for the sauce into a small bowl, cover with water and leave to soak overnight.

The next day, make the sauce. Drain the soaked apricots and chop very finely. Melt the butter in a medium-sized pan. Add the onions and fry for 5–7 minutes until soft and lightly browned. Add the red chilli, curry powder and turmeric and fry for another minute.

Add the chopped apricots, stock and sugar, bring the mixture to the boil and leave it to simmer for 5 minutes. Stir in the vinegar and salt and leave it to go cold. Then stir the sauce into the marinating meat with the rest of the dried apricots, cover and leave for another 2 hours.

Meanwhile, peel the onions leaving the root intact. Cut each one into wedges through the root so that the slices stay together in one piece.

Thread the cubes of lamb, dried apricots and onion wedges on to the skewers. Pour the leftover marinade into a pan, bring it to the boil and leave it to simmer for 2 minutes. Mix the cornflour with 1 tablespoon of cold water, stir it into the sauce and simmer for a couple of minutes until very slightly thickened. Keep warm.

Barbecue the kebabs over medium-hot coals for 10–15 minutes, turning now and then, until nicely browned but still pink and juicy in the centre. Serve with the apricot sauce.

Lamb Steaks with Tarragon Bean Parcels

Lamb steaks cut from a small leg of lamb cook fantastically on the barbecue. I have also cooked alongside them little foil parcels of green beans, flavoured with fresh tarragon. Although the beans lose that lovely green colour when cooked this way they still taste absolutely wonderful.

Serves 4
4 x 225 g (8 oz) leg lamb steaks
2 garlic cloves
4 shallots, finely chopped
2 tablespoons olive oil
75 ml (3 fl oz) red wine
salt and freshly ground black pepper
For the bean parcels:
450 g (1 lb) French beans, topped, tailed and
  halved
50 g (2 oz) butter, melted
1 garlic clove, very finely chopped
1 tablespoon chopped fresh tarragon
2 plum tomatoes, skinned, seeded and chopped

Make small, deep incisions here and there over both sides of the lamb steaks. Cut one of the garlic cloves into thin slivers and push one piece into each cut.
Crush the second clove of garlic into a large, shallow non-metallic dish and mix in the shallots, oil, wine and some seasoning.
Add the lamb steaks to the dish, cover and leave to marinate for 2 hours at room temperature or overnight in the fridge, turning them every now and then.
For the bean parcels, simply mix together all the ingredients with some seasoning in a bowl. Divide between 4 x 30 cm (12 in) squares of extra-thick foil and pinch the edges together into well-sealed parcels.
Barbecue the bean parcels over medium-hot coals for 10 minutes. Then add the lamb to the rack and cook for a further 15 minutes, turning the lamb once. You can either tip the beans out of the foil or leave them in their parcels to serve alongside the lamb.

Moroccan Spiced Lamb Kebabs

The spices in this dish are very typical of those found all over Northern Africa. Harissa paste is a fiery red chilli paste from this region but you can replace it with minced red chilli from a jar if you wish. This one really creeps up on you – an absolute winner everytime.

Serves 4
900 g (2 lb) boned shoulder or leg of lamb
3 tablespoons olive oil
2 tablespoons lemon juice
1 teaspoon ground cumin
1 teaspoon ground coriander
½ teaspoon ground turmeric
½ tablespoon paprika
1 garlic clove, crushed
1 teaspoon harissa paste
1 small red onion
1 small lemon
salt and freshly ground black pepper

4 x 30 cm (12 in) flat metal skewers

Trim any excess fat off the outside of the lamb and then cut it into roughly 5 cm (2 in) chunks. Place it into a bowl with the olive oil, lemon juice, spices, garlic, harissa paste and some seasoning and mix together well. Cover and leave to marinate at room temperature for 2 hours or overnight in the fridge.
Peel the onion, leaving the root end intact and then cut it into 8 wedges, so that the slices of onion stay together at the root. Cut each lemon into 8 wedges.
Thread the lamb, lemon and onion wedges alternately on to the skewers and barbecue over medium-hot coals for about 10–15 minutes, turning them now and then, until they are nicely browned on the outside but still pink in the centre. These would be nice served with the either the Spicy Casablanca Couscous on page 143 or the Tangier Mint Tabbouleh Salad on page 138.

OPPOSITE Moroccan Spiced Lamb Kebabs with Spicy Casablanca Couscous (see page 143)

Mighty Mexican Lamb or Beef Fajitas

In Mexican restaurants, thin strips of beef, lamb or chicken, peppers and onions are cooked on a cast-iron skillet and brought sizzling to the table with a pile of warm flour tortillas, tomato salsa, lettuce and soured cream. Here I have marinated one large piece of meat which keeps it more moist during cooking, but it is still served with the traditional accompaniments. This is a great dish to serve up to a large number of people.

Serves 6–8
900 g (2 lb) thick piece of flank steak or boned
  leg of lamb
2 red peppers
2 yellow peppers
2 green peppers
2 large onions
sunflower oil for brushing
For the marinade:
3 garlic cloves, crushed
juice of 2 limes
4 tablespoons tequila
3 tablespoons olive oil
1 tablespoon chilli powder
1 tablespoon paprika
1 teaspoon ground cumin
1 teaspoon dried oregano
salt and freshly ground black pepper
To serve:
12–16 flour tortillas
1 small iceberg lettuce, very finely shredded
1 quantity Mexican Aztec Salsa (see page 34)
300 ml (10 fl oz) soured cream

6–8 x 25 cm (10 in) flat metal skewers

Place the steak or lamb into a large shallow dish. Mix together the marinade ingredients, pour over the meat, cover and leave to marinate for 2 hours at room temperature or up to 24 hours in the fridge.

Cut the peppers in half, remove the seeds and cut across into 1 cm (½ in) thick slices. Peel the onions, leaving the root end intact and cut each one into thin wedges through the root so that the slices stay together in one piece.

Thread the pepper slices and the onion wedges on to parallel pairs of skewers so that they lie across the two like the rungs of a ladder. This will make it easier to turn them during cooking.

Just before cooking, sprinkle each of the tortillas with a little water, stack 6 or 8 into a pile and wrap up into 2 foil parcels. Place the lettuce, salsa and soured cream into 3 serving bowls.

Lift the steak out of the marinade and barbecue over medium-hot coals for about 20 minutes for medium-rare, turning and basting with the leftover marinade now and then.

At the same time, brush the peppers and onions with a little oil and barbecue them alongside the steak for 10–15 minutes, turning once.

When the steak is ready, lift it onto a board, cover with a sheet of foil and leave to rest for 5 minutes.

Meanwhile, rest the foil tortilla parcels to the side of the barbecue and leave for 5 minutes to warm through.

When the vegetables are cooked, remove them from the grill and slide them off the skewers into another serving bowl.

Carve the steak into thin slices, arrange it on a warmed serving plate and instruct your guests to place some lettuce, steak, peppers, onions, salsa and soured cream down the centre of a tortilla. Roll it up tightly and eat straight away.

Mari-Masala Lamb Fillets

If you marinate any meat in yoghurt it becomes unbelievably tender and when you add plenty of spices, garlic and chilli, it's incredibly tasty too. Here I have used little, sweet lamb fillets served with fried onions flavoured with mustard seeds, warmed naan bread, a tomato salad and some minty yoghurt sauce for a delicious meal in one.

Serves 4

4 x 175 g (6 oz) OR 2 x 350g (12 oz) lamb fillets, trimmed
1 tablespoon garam masala or mild curry paste
pinch of ground cardamom (optional)
½ teaspoon salt
5 garlic cloves, crushed
1 tablespoon harissa paste or minced red chilli from a jar
1 teaspoon lemon juice
200 g (7 oz) Greek natural yoghurt
2 tablespoons sunflower oil
1 tablespoon black mustard seeds
3 onions, thinly sliced
salt and freshly ground black pepper
To serve:
4 tomatoes, sliced
1 small red onion, thinly sliced into rings
1 teaspoon roasted cumin seeds (page 19)
1 teaspoon lemon juice
4 mini naan bread or 2 large breads, cut in half lengthways
1 quantity Mellow Minty Yoghurt Sauce (page 30)

Mix the garam masala or curry paste, ground cardamom, salt, 3 crushed garlic cloves, harissa or red chilli paste and lemon juice into the yoghurt.
Lightly score the outside of the lamb fillets, lay them in a shallow non-metallic dish and pour over the yoghurt mixture. Rub the mixture into the lamb really well, cover and leave to marinate at room temperature for 1 hour or overnight in the fridge.
Heat the oil in a large pan. Add the mustard seeds and as soon as they start to pop, add the onions and fry over a medium heat, stirring now and then, until they are richly golden. Stir in the rest of the garlic, season with a little salt and pepper and cook for 2–3 minutes. Set aside and keep warm.
Layer the tomatoes and red onions in a shallow dish, sprinkling each layer with some of the roasted cumin seeds, lemon juice, salt and

pepper. Set to one side.
Cook the marinated fillets over medium-hot coals for 4–5 minutes on each side for medium-rare lamb.
Meanwhile, sprinkle the naan bread on both sides with a little water and leave to the side of the barbecue for 2–3 minutes, turning once, until heated through.
Remove the lamb fillets to a board and cut diagonally into thick slices. Place the lamb, naan bread and fried onions on to 4 plates and serve with the tomato salad and a spoonful of the minty yoghurt sauce. I bet there'll be plenty of people with a dribble of creamy yoghurt on their chins!

Lively Liver, Bacon and Onion Kebabs

This is a much loved combination of flavours and it works just as well cooked on a barbecue. Just be really careful that you don't overcook the liver. Buy it in a thick slice so that you can cut it into chunky pieces which will not dry out as easily during cooking. Remember, it's far better juicy than dry.

Serves 4

350 g (12 oz) thick slice of lambs' liver
8 small shallots
½ tablespoon chopped fresh parsley
½ tablespoon chopped fresh sage
10 rashers rindless streaky bacon, halved
salt and pepper

4 x 25 cm (10 in) flat metal skewers

Drop the peeled shallots into a pan of boiling water and cook for about 3 minutes until just tender. Drain and refresh under cold water and then cut each one in half through the root.
Cut the liver into 4 cm (1½ in) pieces, place into a bowl and add the parsley, sage and plenty of seasoning. Toss everything together so that the herbs stick to the outside of the liver. Stretch each piece of bacon with the back of a knife and then warp around a piece of liver.
Thread the liver and shallots alternately on to the skewers and barbecue over medium-hot coals for 10 minutes, turning now and then, until the bacon is crisp but the liver is still juicy in the centre.

Butterflied Studded Leg of Lamb

I cooked this recipe whilst I was in South Africa, using their local speciality called Karoo lamb. It has a very distinctive herby flavour which comes from the herby pastures on which the sheep are raised. You can of course use any leg of lamb, although Welsh lamb is often considered to be our best, and the imported chilled New Zealand lamb is very good too. You will need to remember to make the citrus oil the day before the barbecue. Go on, get studding.

Serves 6–8

2–2.5 kg (4–4½ lb) leg of lamb
12 x 25 cm (10 in) stalks of woody rosemary
3 fat garlic cloves
6–8 very small garlic cloves (optional)
4 tablespoons medium dry sherry
salt and freshly ground black pepper

For the citrus oil:
1 lemon
1 small orange
1 large lime
300 ml (10 fl oz) olive oil
½ teaspoon black peppercorns

For the onion and rosemary skewers:
18 small onions
icing sugar for dusting

You will first need to make the citrus oil so that it has plenty of time to mature. Thinly pare the zest off the lemon, orange and lime and place it into a small pan with the oil and the peppercorns. Leave over a very gentle heat for about 5 minutes and then remove, pour into a heatproof glass bottle and leave to cool completely. Seal and leave for 24 hours.

To bone the leg of lamb, find the place where the long bone running down the length of the leg appears to run quite close to the surface. Split open the meat along that bone and carefully peel it back from either side. At the fatter end of the leg there is a small group of smaller bones. Continue to cut the meat away from these bones until you have completely opened up the leg and can lift them out.

You should now have a piece of meat shaped like butterfly wings, hence the name. Trim off any excess fat and neaten it up into a piece of meat about 4–5 cm (1½–2 in) thick all over. If this all sounds a bit too much, just get your butcher to do it for you!

Break the leaves off 2 of the stalks of rosemary in small clusters and strip the remaining pieces clean for the onion skewers. Leave the woody stalks to soak in cold water for 30 minutes. Cut the garlic into long thin slivers.

Make small, deep incisions all over both sides of the lamb and push in the sprigs of rosemary and slivers of garlic. (You could get small whole cloves in too if you're keen on garlic.)

Drizzle over the sherry, some of the citrus oil and season well with salt and pepper. Barbecue over medium-hot coals for about 40 minutes for medium-rare lamb, turning occasionally.

Meanwhile, cut the onions in half and thread 3 halves on to each rosemary stalk. Brush them with some of the citrus oil and place them on to the barbecue alongside the lamb. Dust with the icing sugar and cook for 15–20 minutes, turning every now and then.

Lift the lamb on to a board, cover with a sheet of foil and leave to rest for 5 minutes while the onion skewers finish cooking. Then carve it into thin slices and serve with the onions and the Fire-roasted Red Pepper and Nectarine Salad on page 143 if you wish.

OPPOSITE Studded Butterflied Leg of Lamb with Fire-roasted Red Pepper and Nectarine Salad (see page 143)

BEEF

Clustered Peppered Minute Steaks with Béarnaise Sauce

A minute steak is simply a 2.5 cm (1 in) thick piece of steak which has been flattened out slightly so that it cooks through very quickly. So you don't break the meat apart too much, it is better to flatten it out with the palm of your hand, rather than beating it to death with a mallet or rolling pin.

Serves 6
6 x 90 g (3½ oz) fillet, rump or sirloin steaks
2 tablespoons black peppercorns
1 tablespoon sunflower oil or melted butter
salt and freshly ground black pepper
For the béarnaise sauce:
1 large or 2 smaller shallots, very finely chopped
6 black peppercorns, crushed
2 tablespoons white wine vinegar
150 ml (5 fl oz) dry white wine
175 g (6 oz) butter
3 medium egg yolks
1 teaspoon English mustard powder
1 tablespoon chopped fresh tarragon

To prepare the steaks, lay them between 2 large sheets of clingfilm or non-stick baking parchment and flatten them out with the palm of your hand until they are about 5 mm (¼ in) thick.
Coarsely crush the peppercorns in a pestle and mortar or in a mug using the end of a rolling pin. Tip the pepper into a tea strainer or very fine sieve and give it a good shake to remove all the very fine powder – you only want the coarser grains.

Brush the steaks with a little oil or melted butter and then lightly sprinkle about ½ teaspoon of the crushed pepper on to both sides of each steak. Press it on so that it sticks and then set aside while you make the sauce.
Fill a small thermos flask which will hold at least 600 ml (1 pint) with boiling hot water, seal and set to one side.
Put the shallots, black peppercorns, vinegar and white wine into a small pan and boil vigorously until reduced to about 3 tablespoons.
Put the butter into another pan and leave it to melt and slowly come to the boil.
Put the egg yolks, mustard powder and a pinch of salt into a food processor and give them a quick whizz. Strain in the hot wine and vinegar mixture and whizz once more.
With the motor still running, very slowly pour the hot melted butter through the lid of the goblet – the mixture will gradually thicken. Pour the sauce into a jug and stir in the chopped tarragon and a little salt and pepper to taste.
Drain the water out of the flask, dry it out with a cloth and then pour in the sauce and screw on the lid. This will now keep warm for up to 45 minutes.
Barbecue the steaks for just 1 minute on each side. Season them with a pinch of salt and serve with the béarnaise sauce.

Alan and Andy's Aussie Steaks

Another recipe prepared in stunning Australia and eaten by Alan, the cameraman, and Andy, the sound engineer quicker than you can say 'fair dinkum'. These steaks really are quite delicious and mighty satisfying too. If they're not in the supermarket ask at the customer service desk or go to a good butchers' shop.

Serves 4
4 x 275 g (10 oz) T-Bone steaks, cut about
   2.5–4 cm (1–1½ in) thick
1 x 75 cl bottle Australian red wine such as a
   Shiraz
1 whole head of garlic
1 tablespoon mixed peppercorns (black, white,
   pink and green)
1 tablespoon fresh rosemary leaves
leaves from 3–4 sprigs of fresh thyme
salt and freshly ground black pepper

Pour half the bottle of wine into a large, shallow, non-metallic dish. Cut the garlic horizontally in half and add to the wine.
Coarsely crush the peppercorns in a pestle and mortar or in a mug using the end of a rolling pin and add to the wine with the rosemary and thyme leaves.
Add the steaks, turn once or twice in the mixture and leave to marinate for 2 hours at room temperature or up to 24 hours in the fridge, remembering to turn them every now and then.
Lift the steaks out of the marinade and shake off any excess.
Barbecue over medium-hot coals for 3–4 minutes each side for rare, 4–6 minutes for medium or about 7 minutes each side for well done. This will really depend on how thick your steaks are and how hot the coals are, so keep testing them until they are done to your liking.
Season on both sides with some salt and pepper and serve. These would be really nice served with the Shallot, Mustard and Black Peppercorn Butter on page 31. Now, might I suggest a few glasses of the remaining Shiraz wine... ooooh.

Rub 'n' Brush Barbecued Devilled Beef

This very English spicy mixture, usually containing mustard and cayenne pepper, dates back to the Victorian era and it makes an excellent marinade for steak. The meat is first rubbed with a dry mixture and then brushed with a wet mixture just before cooking. Sounds exciting, looks exciting, tastes superb.

Serves 4
4 x 175–225 g (6–8 oz) fillet or sirloin steaks, cut
   about 2.5–4 cm (1–1½ in) thick
2 teaspoons English mustard powder
¼ teaspoon ground allspice
½ teaspoon ground black pepper
½ teaspoon salt
150 g (5 oz) light soft brown sugar
2 tablespoons tomato ketchup
2 tablespoons Worcestershire sauce
1 tablespoon made English mustard (or mustard
   powder mixed to a paste with a little water)
½ teaspoon Tabasco sauce
2 tablespoons white wine vinegar
1 teaspoon paprika

Mix the English mustard powder, ground allspice, black pepper, salt and 1 tablespoon of the sugar together in a small bowl. In another bowl mix the remaining sugar with the rest of the ingredients into a smooth paste.
Rub the dry spiced sugar mixture on to both sides of the steaks and set them aside for at least 45 minutes or until you are ready to cook.
Brush the steaks with some of the devilled glaze and barbecue over medium-hot coals for about 8 minutes for medium-rare steak, turning and basting them with more of the devilled mixture now and then.

Pai-Thai Beef Salad

The people of Thailand and neighbouring countries are very fond of those semi-clear, slightly spicy sauces and this one is drizzled over thin slices of tender, medium-rare steak and served with a crunchy lettuce salad. You will need to ask your butcher to cut the steak especially for you but it will have been worth the extra journey, I promise!

Serves 4
750 g (1½ lb) piece of sirloin steak, cut 5 cm (2 in) thick
juice of 1 lime
2 teaspoons palm or light muscovado sugar
salt and ground Sichuan pepper
For the salad:
1 crisp lettuce such as Cos, Romaine or iceberg
½ cucumber
3 tomatoes, skinned, quartered and seeded
1 red onion, halved and thinly sliced
leaves from a small bunch or fresh coriander
For the dressing
4 tablespoons lime juice
4 tablespoons Thai fish sauce
1–2 red birdseye chillies, seeded and thinly sliced
1 stalk of lemongrass, outer leaves removed and the core very finely chopped
2 garlic cloves, very finely chopped
2 spring onions, trimmed and very thinly sliced
2 tablespoons chopped fresh mint
1 tablespoon palm or light muscovado sugar

Break the lettuce for the salad into leaves, wash and dry well. Tear them into large pieces and place into a salad bowl.
Peel the cucumber, cut it in half lengthways and scoop out the seeds with a teaspoon. Slice across into thin half-moons.
Cut the tomatoes into thin crescent-shaped strips.
Add the cucumber, tomatoes, red onion and coriander leaves to the lettuce and toss together lightly. Spread over the base of a large oval serving plate and set aside in the fridge to chill.
Mix together all the ingredients for the dressing and set aside.
Sprinkle the steak on both sides with the lime juice and sugar and then season with some salt and Sichuan pepper.
Barbecue over medium-hot coals for 25–30 minutes, turning frequently, until well browned on the outside but still rare and juicy in the centre. Remove to a board, cover with a sheet of foil and leave to rest for 10 minutes.
Carve the steak into thin slices and arrange in the centre of the chilled salad leaves. Spoon over the dressing and serve immediately.

OPPOSITE Pad-Thai Beef Salad

Beef 'Bourguignon' Kebabs

For these kebabs I've simply taken all the essential ingredients from that classic French stew and threaded them on to skewers ready for barbecuing. They take a little time to prepare, but they can be done in advance and are very quick to cook once you're ready to eat.

Serves 6
900 g (2 lb) sirloin or rump steak, cut into 4 cm (1½ in) cubes
225 g (8 oz) rindless smoked streaky bacon
18 button onions, peeled
24 button mushrooms, wiped
olive oil for brushing
salt and freshly ground black pepper
For the marinade:
5 tablespoon red wine
3 tablespoons olive oil
1 tablespoon tomato purée
2 shallots, finely chopped
2 garlic cloves, crushed
2 tablespoons chopped fresh parsley
12 small fresh bay leaves

12 x 25 cm (10 in) flat metal skewers

Mix together the ingredients for the marinade and pour it into a non-metallic dish. Stir in the steak, cover and leave to marinate at room temperature for 2 hours or in the fridge overnight.
The next day stretch the bacon rashers on a board with the back of a knife. Cut each rasher in half and roll up tightly.
Drop the button onions into a pan of boiling water and cook for 2–3 minutes until just tender. Drain and refresh under cold water.
Thread the cubes of beef, the onions, bacon rolls, mushrooms and bay leaves from the marinade alternately on to the skewers. Brush the mushrooms and the onions with a little extra olive oil and then season the kebabs well with salt and pepper.
Barbecue the kebabs over medium-hot coals for 6 minutes, turning and basting with the leftover marinade now and then.

Beef Peppa-feta Rolls

These one person-sized parcels are shaped a little bit like beef olives. They are made from thin slices of steak which are stuffed, rolled up and in this case secured with fine skewers or cocktail sticks instead of string. Make sure that you turn them around quite a bit during cooking so that they cook right through to the centre.

Serves 4
4 x 150 g (5 oz) sirloin steaks
2 red peppers
100 g (4 oz) feta cheese, sliced
25 g (1 oz) pitted black olives, sliced
1 beef tomato, skinned, seeded and cut into strips
2 tablespoons chopped fresh basil
1 tablespoon olive oil

4 fine metal trussing skewers or cocktail sticks soaked in cold water for 30 minutes

Barbecue or grill the peppers over medium-hot coals for about 20 minutes, turning now and then, until the skins are quite black all over. Drop them into a plastic bag, seal tightly and leave to cool.
Cut the peppers in half and remove the seeds. Then turn over each piece and gently scrape away all the charred skin with a small sharp knife.
Place the steaks between two large pieces of clingfilm or non-stick baking parchment and carefully flatten them until they are about 5 mm (¼ in) thick, taking care not to break the meat apart when you're doing this. You don't want any holes!
Lay the steaks out flat on a board and cover each one with one flat piece of grilled red pepper.
Now place some cheese, black olives, tomatoes and chopped basil along one short edge of each steak. Roll up tightly and secure in place with skewers or cocktail sticks.
Brush the outside of the rolls with the oil and barbecue over medium- hot coals for 8–10 minutes, turning now and then, until browned all over and cooked through in the centre.

Surf and Turf Barbecue Skewers

This unusually named dish comes from Australia, where they serve prawns from the 'surf' or sea, together with steak reared on the 'turf'. Unlikely as it may seem, they actually go together really well, especially when they are both smothered with a yummy garlic and parsley butter. Now, anyone for a swim, or a stroll in the grass?

Serves 4
350 g (12 oz) piece of sirloin or rump steak, cut 2.5 cm (1 in) thick
12 headless raw tiger prawns
3 tablespoons olive oil
2 garlic cloves, crushed
1 teaspoon paprika
¼ teaspoon Tabasco sauce
½ teaspoon Worcestershire sauce
salt and freshly ground black pepper
For the garlic and parsley butter:
50 g (2 oz) butter
2 garlic cloves, crushed
2 tablespoons chopped fresh parsley
finely grated zest of ½ lemon
1 tablespoon lemon juice

4 x 25 cm (10 in) bamboo skewers, soaked in cold water for
  30 minutes

Cut the steak into roughly 16 x 2.5 cm (1 in) cubes. Peel the prawns, leaving the last tail segment in place.
Mix the olive oil with the garlic, paprika, Tabasco, Worcestershire sauce and plenty of salt and pepper. Dip the prawns into the marinade, lift out and set aside on a plate.
Stir the cubes of steak into the marinade and leave for 15 minutes.
Thread 4 pieces of steak and 3 prawns alternately on to the skewers and barbecue over medium-hot coals for 5–10 minutes, turning every now and then, until the steak is done to your liking and the prawns are just cooked through.
Meanwhile, put the butter and garlic into a small pan and leave to the side of the barbecue to melt. Add the chopped parsley, lemon zest and lemon juice.
As soon as the kebabs are cooked, lift them onto 4 plates, spoon over the garlic butter and serve with the Damper Beer Bread on page 151 if you wish.

OPPOSITE Surf and Turf Barbecue Skewers with Damper Beer Bread
(see page 151)

Spiced Indian Kofta

This mixture can either be divided into small pieces and shaped around wooden skewers or you could simply flatten them into disc-like patties as a nice change from the usual beefburger.

Serves 4
450 g (1 lb) lean minced beef
1 garlic clove, crushed
2.5 cm (1 in) fresh root ginger, peeled and finely grated
2 spring onions, trimmed and finely chopped
½ teaspoon salt
1 teaspoon ground cumin
1 teaspoon ground coriander
½ teaspoon garam masala
pinch of cayenne pepper
3 tablespoons chopped fresh coriander
1 green chilli, seeded and very finely chopped
3 tablespoons Greek natural yoghurt
a little sunflower oil for brushing
lemon wedges and extra Greek natural yoghurt to serve

8 x 15 cm (6 in) bamboo skewers, soaked in cold water for 30
   minutes

Simply put everything except the oil for brushing into a bowl and mix it together well with your hands.
Divide the mixture into 8 and then shape each piece into a long sausage around each skewer.
Brush the koftas with a little oil and barbecue over medium-hot coals for 8–10 minutes, turning now and then, until lightly browned and cooked through. Serve with the lemon wedges and the natural yoghurt, and maybe some naan bread warmed through on the barbecue (see page 75).

VARIATION
Substitute minced lamb for the minced beef and chopped mint for the chopped coriander. Divide the mixture into 16 and shape into little egg-shaped balls around 1 cm (½ in) cubes of feta cheese (you will need to buy about 100 g (4 oz)). Thread the balls on to 4 soaked 25 cm (10 in) bamboo skewers before cooking and serve with perhaps the Mellow Minty Yoghurt Sauce on page 30 and the Garlic Pitta Fingers on page 150.

Mustard and Sugar-coated Beef with Soured Cream and Horseradish Dip

For a quick barbecued alternative to roast beef and horseradish sauce this is the perfect recipe. Come Sunday, Monday, Tuesday, Wednesday, Thursday, Friday, Saturday, it'll be gone. (Reminds me of a song...)

Serves 4
450 g (1 lh) fillet steak, cut into
  4 cm (1 ½ in) cubes
2 tablespoons light soft brown sugar
2 teaspoons English mustard powder
salt and freshly ground black pepper
For the dip:
150 ml (5 fl oz) soured cream
1–2 tablespoons horseradish sauce
  (not creamed horseradish)
1 teaspoon snipped fresh chives

4 x 25 cm (10 in) flat metal skewers

Mix the soured cream with the horseradish sauce and chives and set aside.
Place the cubes of steak into a shallow dish and season with a little salt and pepper.
Mix the sugar and mustard powder together and sprinkle over the beef, turning the pieces as you go so that they all get an even coating.
Thread the steak on to the skewers and barbecue over medium-hot coals for 4–5 minutes, turning now and then, until the sugar has caramelized but the steak is still rare in the centre. Serve with the horseradish and soured cream dip and start licking the lips.

SAUSAGES & BURGERS

Classic Brilliant Beefburgers

A really good beefburger has to be made from really good minced beef. If you can, ask a butcher to mince some rump, blade or chuck steak for you but make sure that it has at least a 20 per cent fat content as this will in effect make them self-basting and prevent them from drying out during cooking. Otherwise buy ordinary minced beef from the supermarket, but don't buy extra-lean mince because they will become as tough as old boots during cooking. I like to serve these up in soft baps or muffins with an all-in-one lettuce-mayonnaise topping that will hopefully stay put in the bun while you eat it!

Serves 4
750 g (1½ lb) minced beef
2 garlic cloves, crushed
1 small onion, finely chopped
2 tablespoons double cream
1 tablespoon chopped fresh parsley
salt and freshly ground black pepper
For the lettuce mayonnaise:
2 tablespoons mayonnaise
100 g (4 oz) iceberg lettuce, finely shredded
50 g (2 oz) cocktail gherkins, finely chopped
2 tablespoons finely chopped onion
1 teaspoon mild American-style mustard
To serve:
4 sesame bread rolls or baps, halved
2 tomatoes, thinly sliced

Simply mix all the ingredients for the burgers together in a bowl or blitz quickly in a food processor until the meat starts to hold together.
Divide the mixture into 4 and shape into 10 cm (4 in) flat discs, either by hand or by pressing the mixture into a metal pastry cutter.
Brush the burgers with a little oil and barbecue over medium-hot coals for about 5 minutes on each side for medium.
Meanwhile for the topping, mix the mayonnaise with the rest of the ingredients and season to taste with a little salt and pepper.
To serve, lightly toast the cut sides of the rolls on the barbecue for 1–2 minutes. Cover the bottom half with a couple of slices of tomato and then sit the burger on top. Drop a spoonful of the lettuce mayonnaise on top, cover with the top half of the bun and eat straight away.

VARIATIONS
Barbecue Beefburgers Mix 2–3 tablespoons of the My Classic Barbecue Sauce (page 28) into the basic mixture and serve in buns with Ainsley's Ultimate Creole Cabbage Salad (page 147).

Chilli Cheeseburgers Cut 50 g (2 oz) of Cheddar into 4 cubes. Mix 1 seeded and chopped red chilli and 1 tablespoon of chopped fresh parsley into the basic mixture and shape around each piece of cheese. Serve in buns with some Fire-roasted Red Pepper Guacamole (see page 42) or Mexican Aztec Salsa (see page 34) and soured cream.

Pork and Apple Burgers Use minced pork instead of beef and add 1 peeled and grated Cox's apple and 1 tablespoon of chopped fresh sage. Barbecue over medium-hot coals for 6–7 minutes on each side until well done and serve in buns with lettuce and a dollop of wholegrain mustard mayonnaise.

Pork and Mozzarella Burgers Mix 1 tablespoon of chopped fresh oregano and 1 tablespoon of sundried tomato paste with the minced pork and shape around 15 g (½ oz) cubes of Mozzarella. Barbecue over medium-hot coals for 6–7 minutes on each side until well done and serve in buns with salad and garlic mayonnaise.

Lamb Tikka Burgers Use minced lamb instead of beef and mix in ¼ teaspoon each of ground coriander and cumin, cayenne pepper, turmeric powder, 1 crushed garlic clove and 1 teaspoon of grated ginger. Barbecue over medium-hot coals for 5–6 minutes on each side and serve in buns or mini naan breads with lettuce, tomatoes, mango chutney and Mellow Minty Yoghurt Sauce (see page 30).

Chicken and Bacon Burgers Use minced chicken instead of beef and add 6 very finely chopped rashers of rindless streaky bacon. Barbecue over medium-hot coals for 6–7 minutes on each side until well done and serve in buns with lettuce, extra grilled bacon, sliced tomatoes and mayonnaise.

Classic Brilliant Beefburger with My Classic Barbecue Sauce (see page 28) and New Potato Salad with Gherkins, Chives and Soured Cream (see page 142)

Boss Barbecue Bangers

Here is a very simple but very tasty way of turning barbecued sausages into something a little different. The sausages are started off under the grill before they're stuffed so that they only take a few minutes to cook through when you're ready.

Serves 8
900 g (2 lb) good quality meaty pork sausages or
    jumbo frankfurters
75 g (3 oz) cheese such as Cheddar, Gouda or
    Gruyère
8 no-need-to-soak prunes
225 g (8 oz) rindless streaky bacon

Lightly brown the sausages under the grill, turning now and then, for about 5 minutes until half cooked. Set aside and leave to go cold.
Cut a slit in each sausage and stuff half of them with the cheese and the other half with the prunes. The frankfurters taste best with just the cheese.
Stretch the rashers of bacon on a chopping board with the back of a knife and then wind 1 rasher around each sausage, leaving gaps in between so that the filling shows through. These can now be set aside until you are ready to cook them.
Barbecue the 'bangers' over medium-hot coals for about 7 minutes, turning now and then, until the bacon is crisp and the cheese has melted.

Venison Sausages with Red Onion Marmalade

I've suggested venison sausages here but you could use absolutely any well-flavoured, good quality sausage. Most supermarkets now have a great selection or you could seek out a local butcher who makes his own.

Serves 6
12 venison sausages
For the red onion marmalade:
25 g (1 oz) butter
450 g (1 lb) red onions, halved and sliced
1 tablespoon light soft brown sugar
250 ml (8 fl oz) red wine
50 ml (2 fl oz) red wine vinegar
salt and freshly ground black pepper

For the onion marmalade, melt the butter in a medium-sized pan.
Add the onions and sugar and cook over a medium heat, stirring, until soft and lightly caramelized.
Add the wine and vinegar and leave to cook for about another 10 minutes until all the liquid has evaporated and the onions are very soft.
Season with salt and pepper and keep hot.
Pierce the sausages here and there with a fine skewer and barbecue over medium-hot coals for 8–10 minutes, turning now and then, until golden. Serve with the red onion marmalade.

Chicken and Sausage Hot Dogs with Fried Onions

Here's a twist on that well-known British street food. It tastes much better too, thanks to the tangy barbecue sauce that's used to flavour the chicken and frankfurters. Kids love 'em.

Serves 4

3 chicken breast fillets
4 jumbo frankfurters
75 g (3 oz) butter
1 tablespoon oil
3 onions, thinly sliced
1 teaspoon granulated sugar
120 ml (4 fl oz) spicy tomato ketchup
1 tablespoon English mustard
1 tablespoon tomato purée
1 tablespoon Worcestershire sauce
¼ teaspoon barbecue seasoning
4 hot dog rolls

4 x 30 cm (12 in) bamboo skewers soaked in cold water for 30 minutes

Heat 25 g (1 oz) of the butter and the oil in a medium-sized pan. Add the onions and fry over a gentle heat for 15 minutes, stirring now and then until very soft. Add the sugar and cook for another 15 minutes, still stirring until they have lightly caramelized. Set aside and keep warm.

Cut each chicken fillet lengthways into 4 strips and cut each frankfurter into 4 pieces.

Roll each piece of chicken up into a spiral. Thread 3 pieces of chicken and 4 pieces of frankfurter alternately on to each skewer.

Melt the rest of the butter in a small pan. Stir in the tomato ketchup, mustard, tomato purée, Worcestershire sauce and barbecue seasoning.

Brush the kebabs liberally with the sauce and barbecue over medium-hot coals for about 20 minutes, turning and basting with the leftover sauce now and then. Brush with the rest of the barbecue sauce right at the end of cooking so that they are nice and gooey.

To serve, halve the hot dog rolls and spoon in some of the fried onions. Rest a kebab on top of the onions, close the bun tightly and slide out the skewers.

Herby Home-made Sausagemeat Patties

These are a bit like home made sausages, without the skins. They are mega-quick to make and taste absolutely fab with the Speedy Tomato and Red Pepper Chutney on page 36, served in buns if you like.

Serves 4

750 g (1½ lb) good quality
   pork sausagemeat
3 shallots or ½ small onion,
   very finely chopped
1 tablespoon chopped fresh
   marjoram or oregano
2 teaspoons chopped fresh
   thyme or sage
1½ tablespoons Dijon mustard
salt and freshly ground black pepper

Just mix all the ingredients together in a bowl and then roughly shape the mixture into 8 x 10 cm (4 in) cm flat discs – they don't need to be too neat.

Barbecue the patties over medium hot coals for 4 minutes on each side until golden and cooked through in the centre.

Cumberland Sausage Catherine Wheel

Ideal for a bonfire barbie and a great way of cooking enough sausages to feed lots of people without having to spend hours turning over individual ones as they brown. One long string of untwisted sausages is coiled into a spiral and secured in place with skewers like the spokes of a wheel so that it can cooked in one piece. It is then smothered in a spicy tomato sauce and cut into wedges between the skewers to serve. If you've got less people to feed than I've suggested, just use a shorter string of sausage. If you can, go to a butcher and ask him to make you one long untwisted sausage. Otherwise buy a twisted string, untwist it, and squeeze the meat back into the spaces before shaping.

Serves 12–14

1.75 kg (4 lb) untwisted Cumberland pork sausage in one length
1 large onion, very finely chopped
2 garlic cloves, crushed
25 g (1 oz) butter
6 tablespoons tomato ketchup
6 tablespoons sweet chilli sauce (ready-made or see page 28)
1 tablespoon freshly squeezed lemon juice
salt and freshly ground black pepper
1–2 tablespoons chopped fresh parsley

12–14 x 25 cm (10 in) fine metal skewers or bamboo skewers
    soaked in cold water for 30 minutes

Tightly curl the long sausage into a spiral and then push 12–14 fine metal skewers at regular intervals through the sides of the coil into the centre, so that they look like the spokes of a wheel. Set it aside in the fridge until you are ready to start cooking.
For the sauce, fry the onion and the garlic in the butter for 6–7 minutes until soft and lightly browned. Add the tomato ketchup, chilli sauce, lemon juice and seasoning to taste and simmer for 3 minutes until quite thick.
If you can, clamp the 'Catherine wheel' into a hinged wire rack (see page 16) and then barbecue over medium-hot coals for 30 minutes, turning it regularly, until it is lightly browned and cooked through.
Transfer it on to a large serving plate or board, spread it with the spicy tomato sauce and then sprinkle with the chopped parsley. Cut the wheel into wedges between each of the skewers and serve with plenty of crusty bread.

OPPOSITE Cumberland Sausage Catherine Wheel

SEAFOOD

Barbecued Lobster with Three Flavoured Butters

The sight of butter, slowly melting on to freshly barbied lobster and glistening in the sun is something to behold. No wonder it's on the front cover of the book! These butters will make far more than you will need for 4 people but they will keep in the fridge for up to a week and can be frozen for up to 2 months. They would be great served with any grilled fish.

Serves 4
2 x 750g–1 kg (1½–2¼ lb) uncooked lobsters or
    crayfish
2 lemons
salt and freshly ground black pepper
For the tarragon, shallot and white wine butter:
150 ml (5 fl oz) dry white wine
2 shallots, very finely chopped
100 g (4 oz) slightly salted butter, softened
2 tablespoons chopped fresh tarragon
For the caper, garlic and parsley butter:
100 g (4 oz) slightly salted butter, softened
2 garlic cloves, crushed
1 tablespoon drained capers, finely chopped
2 tablespoons chopped fresh flatleaf parsley
For the chilli and orange butter:
100 g (4 oz) slightly salted butter, softened
1½ tablespoons extra virgin olive oil
2 red chillies, seeded and very finely chopped
finely grated rind of ½ large orange

First make the butters. For the tarragon, shallot and white wine butter, put the wine and shallots into a pan and boil vigorously until the wine has almost disappeared. Leave the mixture to cool, then gradually beat it into the butter, followed by the tarragon, ¼ teaspoon of salt and some black pepper.

For the caper, garlic and parsley butter, just mix all the ingredients together and season with ¼ teaspoon of salt and some pepper.

For the chilli and orange butter, mix all the ingredients together with ¼ teaspoon of salt and some pepper. Chill the mixture in the fridge for 10–15 minutes until firm because the oil makes it quite runny.

Now shape and roll all the butters in a piece of clingfilm or non-stick baking parchment to give them a cylindrical shape and chill them in the fridge until firm.

Place the lobsters on to a board, belly-side down and cut them in half lengthways using a large sharp knife. Remove and discard the long dark vein running along the length of the tail. Crack the claws (if there are any) with the back of a large knife or a hammer.

Place the lobsters on to a medium-hot barbecue, flesh-side down, and cook for just 30 seconds to seal in all the juices. Then turn them over and cook for another 6–8 minutes until the flesh has become white and firm and the shells have turned bright red.

Meanwhile, cut each lemon into 8 wedges. Place on the barbecue and cook alongside the lobsters, turning them now and then.

Take a few slices off the butter of your choice and lay them along the flesh of each lobster half. Continue to cook for about another minute until the butter just begins to melt.

Lift the lobsters on to 4 plates and serve at once with the barbecued lemon wedges, plenty of napkins and finger bowls. All go equally well with some crisp Australian Chardonnay. Memories are made of this.

Chargrilled Squid Stuffed with Spinach and Mint

Barbecued food in Greece is always fresh and exciting, and comes in all shapes and sizes, just like squid. For this dish you need squid with pouches about 22 cm (10 in) long. Use your own judgment when it comes to scoring them. If they look a bit thin, don't bother – it's better to do away with the fancy look, rather than have the filling fall out during cooking. Remember, you don't want it falling out!

Serves 4

4 prepared squid, about 22 cm/10 in long
2 tablespoons olive oil
1 small onion, very finely chopped
1 garlic clove, crushed
225 g (8 oz) fresh spinach, washed and large
  stalks removed
2 tablespoons lemon juice
75 g (3 oz) cooked long-grain rice
1 tablespoon chopped fresh mint
300 ml (10 fl oz) passata (sieved tomatoes) or
  sieved fresh tomatoes if you prefer
½ teaspoon caster sugar
2 tablespoons chopped flatleaf parsley
salt and freshly ground black pepper

4 fine metal trussing skewers or cocktail sticks
  soaked in cold water for 30 minutes

Rinse the squid in cold water and drain really well. Score the outside of the pouches in a criss-cross pattern with a small sharp knife if you wish.

Heat 1 tablespoon of the olive oil in a medium-sized pan. Add the onion and garlic and cook gently for 5 minutes until soft and lightly browned. Scoop half the mixture into a bowl and set aside.

Heat the rest of the oil in a large pan. Add the spinach and stir-fry over a high heat until it has wilted into the bottom of the pan. Tip it into a colander or sieve and press out all the excess liquid.

Coarsely chop the spinach and add it to the bowl of onions together with 1 tablespoon of the lemon juice, the cooked rice, the mint and some salt and pepper. Mix together well.

Spoon some of the stuffing into each squid pouch and secure the end with a skewer or cocktail stick. Set aside.

Add the sugar to the remaining fried onions in the pan and cook for another minute or so. Then add the passata and cook for a few minutes until slightly thickened. Stir in the parsley and lemon juice and season to taste with salt and pepper.

Brush the outside of the squid with a little olive oil and season generously, then barbecue over medium-hot coals for about 4–6 minutes, turning now and then, until they are firm and opaque and the stuffing has heated through. Serve with the tomato sauce and a wedge of lemon.

Krungthep Crab and Coconut Cakes

Because the mixture for these little cakes is quite soft, they really need to be cooked on a fine-meshed rack like the one pictured on page 16 or a heavy metal plate that sits on top of the barbecue. This helps to hold them together until they firm up and also stops the mixture from sticking to the bars. Turn them over carefully when cooking, using a spatula or similar utensil.

Serves 4

350 g (12 oz) white crab meat, squeezed to remove any excess moisture

150 g (5 oz) firm white fish such as cod, haddock or coley, skinned and boned

1 tablespoon Thai fish sauce

1 tablespoon oyster sauce

2 garlic cloves, crushed

1 medium egg, beaten

25 g (1oz) unsweetened desiccated coconut

1 red finger chilli, seeded and thinly sliced

4 spring onions, trimmed and thinly sliced

3 tablespoons chopped fresh coriander

sunflower oil for brushing

salt and freshly ground white pepper

1 quantity of Chiang-Mai Thai Dipping Sauce (see page 29) or bottled chilli dipping sauce to serve

Cut the fish into chunks and check that no bones have been left behind. Place the fish into a food processor with the Thai fish sauce, oyster sauce, garlic and some salt and pepper and process for a few seconds until it has formed a rough paste.

Add the crab meat and the egg and process once more for just a few seconds until well blended.

Scrape the mixture into a bowl and mix in the coconut, chilli, spring onions and coriander.

Shape the mixture into 8 x 7.5 cm (3 in) patties. Brush them lightly with some sunflower oil and barbecue over medium-hot coals for 3–4 minutes on each side until golden brown. Serve immediately with the Chiang-Mai Thai Dipping Sauce or bottled chilli dipping sauce.

OPPOSITE Krungthep Crab and Coconut Cakes
BELOW I'm so excited by the gorgeous produce at Chatachak Market, Bangkok.

Portuguese Grilled Sardines

Sometimes the simplest is just the best. These plainly grilled sardines are to be found perched over converted oil-barrel barbecues all over Portugal, served sprinkled with just a little lemon juice and coarse sea salt. Delightfully delicious.

Serves 4
24 fresh sardines
coarse sea salt, lemon wedges and crusty white bread to serve

You will only need to gut the fish if they weigh more than 65 g (2½ oz), so are more than 13 cm (5 in) long. Otherwise you can just leave them as they are.
Rub off the scales under running cold water and then lay them in a fish grilling rack if you wish. This just makes them easier to turn over (all in one go) during cooking.
Barbecue the sardines over medium-hot coals for 3–4 minutes on each side.
Transfer them on to a plate, sprinkle with a little sea salt and serve with the lemon wedges and chunks of fresh crusty white bread.

Jim's Barbecued Tuna and Chips

Most of the tuna caught off the South African coast is exported and nobody knows the reason why. Well, they didn't until they tasted my heavenly fish and chips. The fishermen lapped it up and I have a feeling that the odd one or two will now end up on the barbie, or as they say in South Africa, the braii.

Serves 4

4 x 175 g (6 oz) tuna steaks
4 x 275 g (10 oz) red-skinned sweet potatoes, cut into chunky
  wedges
4 garlic cloves, peeled but left whole
1 teaspoon coarse sea salt
2 long red finger chillies
100 g (4 oz) mayonnaise
1 heaped tablespoon chopped fresh flatleaf parsley
2 tablespoons olive oil
2 tablespoons mixed peppercorns (black, white, pink and green)

Drop the wedges of sweet potato into a pan of lightly salted water and cook for about 10 minutes until just tender.

Meanwhile, put the garlic cloves on to a board and flatten them with the blade of a large knife. Sprinkle over the salt and continue to crush them with the blade of the knife until they form a smooth paste.

Cut the chillies in half, remove the seeds and thinly slice. Stir into the mayonnaise with the garlic and chopped parsley and set to one side.

Drain the sweet potatoes and toss them in the oil until well coated. Arrange them on a meshed wire rack, season with a little salt and and barbecue over medium-hot coals for 6–8 minutes, turning every now and then, until they are lightly golden.

Crush the peppercorns in a pestle and mortar or in a coffee mug using the end of a rolling pin. Press them firmly on to the outside of each tuna steak. Add the tuna to the barbecue and cook for about 2 minutes on each side, or a little longer if you don't like your fish too rare. Season with a little salt.

Pile the chips into the centre of 4 plates and place a tuna steak on top. Add a good dollop of the red chilli mayonnaise to each plate and serve the rest separately in a small bowl. Get dunkin'.

Sally's Salmon Steaks with Fresh Basil Sauce

Unlike pesto sauce, which is quite rich and made with Parmesan and pinenuts, this fresh-tasting sauce is just made with lots of basil, lemon juice and olive oil and it goes perfectly with some simply barbecued salmon.

Serves 4
4 x 200 g (7 oz) salmon steaks
1 tablespoon olive oil

For the fresh basil sauce:
45 g (1½ oz) fresh basil
1 tablespoon freshly squeezed lemon juice
6 tablespoons olive oil
salt and freshly ground black pepper

First of all make the sauce. Set aside 4 sprigs of the basil for a garnish. Remove any large stalks from the remainder and place it into a food processor with the lemon juice and a little salt and pepper.

Turn on the machine and once the basil has blended to a paste, very slowly pour in the olive oil. Check the sauce for seasoning and set to one side.

Brush the salmon steaks on both sides with a little olive oil and season with some salt and black pepper. Barbecue over medium-hot coals for 4–5 minutes on each side until golden on the outside but still moist and juicy in the centre. Serve with the fresh basil sauce and plenty of sparkling white wine. Go on then, champagne all round.

OPPOSITE Sally's Salmon Steaks with Fresh Basil Sauce and Char-roasted New Potato Skewers (see page 126)
BELOW Portuguese Grilled Sardines (see page 98)

Indian Spiced Swordfish Steaks

Swordfish usually comes ready-cut into steaks and is a dark, meaty type of fish which works really well with strong spicy flavours. Take great care not to overcook it because it will dry out very easily.

Serves 4
4 x 175–225 g (6–8 oz) swordfish steaks
3 tablespoons olive oil
1 red onion, finely chopped
1 red finger chilli, seeded and finely chopped
1 green finger chilli, seeded and finely chopped
2 teaspoons mild curry powder
½ teaspoon ground cumin
1 teaspoon cayenne pepper
finely grated zest of 1 lemon
2 tablespoons lemon juice
sea salt

Place the swordfish steaks into a shallow dish.
Heat the oil in a pan, add the onion and the chillies and cook gently for about 6 minutes until soft but not brown.
Add the curry powder, cumin and cayenne pepper and cook for another 2–3 minutes, stirring continuously.
Remove the pan from the heat and stir in the lemon zest, lemon juice and a little salt. Pour the mixture over the swordfish, turn once and leave it to marinate for 1 hour.
Barbecue the steaks over medium-hot coals for about 10 minutes, turning and basting with the leftover marinade now and then, until they are browned on the outside but still moist in the centre.

Ainsley's Mulled Mussels

Whilst having a casual drink with the chef at Cape Town's 'Victoria Junction Hotel' we came up with this simple idea for barbecuing fresh mussels. It's a recipe which combines all the flavours of Cape Cuisine – fresh seafood, fruit and the influence of the subtle spices from Cape Malay – and I'm sure it's on the menu by now.

Serves 4

1.75 kg (4 lb) live mussels
75 g (3 oz) no-need-to-soak dried apricots, thinly sliced
4 tablespoons freshly squeezed orange juice
4 tablespoons freshly squeezed lemon juice
finely grated zest of 1 lemon
8 tablespoons dry white wine
2 garlic cloves, very finely chopped
4 x 2.5 cm (1 in) cinnamon sticks
4 cm (1½ in) fresh root ginger, peeled and thinly sliced
50 g (2 oz) butter
4 tablespoons chopped fresh coriander
4 tablespoons snipped fresh garlic chives or ordinary chives
salt and freshly ground black pepper

8 large squares of turkey-sized foil

Take 2 squares of foil and place one on top of the other. Working your way around the edges, fold the foil over until you have created a boat-shaped container which is about 25 cm (10 in) long, with sides which are at least 4 cm (1½ in) high. Repeat this process to make another 3 boats.

Scrub the mussels and pull out the fibrous beards protruding from between the closed shells. Discard any open mussels which won't close when you lightly tap them on the work surface.

Divide the mussels between the boats and sprinkle over the sliced apricots.

Add 1 tablespoon each of orange and lemon juice, a quarter of the lemon zest, 2 tablespoons of white wine, a quarter of the chopped garlic, a piece of cinnamon and a few slices of ginger to each boat, making sure that everything is pushed in amongst the mussels so that the flavours can permeate them during cooking.

Dot the mussels with 15 g (½ oz) of the butter, season with some salt and pepper and place over a medium-hot barbecue for 10–15 minutes until they have opened. Discard any mussels which remained closed.

Sprinkle some chopped coriander and chives over each boat, remove from the rack on to plates and serve with either ciabatta or foccacia bread, warmed through on the side of the barbecue for a few minutes, to mop up all the juices.

Sweet Chilli King Prawns

Everyone loves to have prawns as a special treat, and these ones are truly special. You could either use large raw king prawns which still have their heads on or the raw, headless tiger prawns which you can now get from most supermarkets, either from the fresh fish counter or the freezer cabinet.

Serves 6
36 raw freshwater king prawns or 72 headless
   raw tiger prawns
3 tablespoons vegetable oil
1 tablespoon clear honey
1 tablespoon chilli sauce
finely grated zest and juice of ½ lime
3–4 garlic cloves, crushed
salt and freshly ground black pepper

6–12 x 25 cm (10 in) fine metal skewers

Peel the prawns leaving the last tail section in place. Make a shallow cut along the curved back of each one and lift out the dark, thread-like intestine.
Mix the rest of the ingredients together in a large bowl. Stir the prawns into the mixture and leave them to marinate in the fridge for up to 2 hours.
Thread the prawns on to the skewers. If you are using king prawns you will be able to thread 6 prawns on to 1 skewer for each person. If you are using tiger prawns you will need to do 2 skewers per person.
Barbecue the prawns over medium-hot coals for about 3–4 minutes, turning them now and then, until they have become firm and opaque. Eat them straight away while they're still hot. Finger licking permitted.

OPPOSITE Sweet Chilli King Prawns with Cool Carrot, Cumin and Lemon Salad (see page 144)
BELOW Oooh, delightfully fresh seafood ... It certainly tickled my fancy. Chatachak Market, Bangkok.

Maddie's Bacon, Sage and Monkfish Wrap with Aioli

'Allo, 'allo, 'allo. Fish and bacon might not be your idea of a good flavour combination but believe me, it's heaven. The firm white flesh of the monkfish is almost meaty once cooked and all this would need is a crisp leaf salad and maybe a few boiled new potatoes to make it into an extra special summertime meal.

Serves 4

2 x 350g (12 oz) monkfish fillets taken from a
   medium-sized 900 g (2 lb) tail
3 tablespoons olive oil
1 tablespoon chopped fresh parsley
1 teaspoon chopped fresh sage
1 teaspoon chopped fresh rosemary
1 teaspoon chopped fresh thyme
salt and freshly ground black pepper
8–10 rashers rindless smoked streaky bacon
6 large fresh sage leaves

For the aioli:

3 garlic cloves, peeled
1–2 teaspoons lemon juice
100 g (4 oz) mayonnaise

4 fine metal trussing skewers or cocktail sticks
   soaked in cold water for 30 minutes

Trim any membrane off the outside of the monkfish fillets and lay them in a shallow dish.

Mix the olive oil with the chopped herbs and some salt and pepper, pour over the monkfish and turn it once or twice in the mixture. Leave to marinate at room temperature for 30 minutes or for up to 2 hours in the fridge.

Meanwhile make the aioli sauce. Lightly crush the cloves of garlic on a board with the blade of a large knife. Sprinkle them with a little salt and then continue to crush them with the side of the blade until they turn into a smooth paste.

Stir the garlic paste and lemon juice into the mayonnaise. Spoon the mixture into a small bowl, cover and chill until required.

Stretch the rashers of bacon on a board with the back of a large knife. Lift the monkfish fillets out of the marinade, lay 3 sage leaves along the top of each one and wrap each fillet in half the bacon rashers, overlapping them slightly. Secure them at either end of each fillet with a skewer or cocktail stick so that they stay in place during cooking.

Barbecue the monkfish over medium-hot coals for 8–10 minutes, turning every now and then, until the bacon is crisp and the fish is only just cooked through in the centre. If you've got a thermometer it should read no more than 50°C/92°F.

Lift each one on to a board, carve them diagonally into thick slices and serve with the aioli sauce.

Citrus Seafood Kebabs

The combination of lemons and limes always goes well with fish. Don't leave the fish to marinate in the fruity mixture for any longer than I've suggested or you will find that the citrus juices will start to 'cook' the fish and make the texture much too soft.

Serves 4

16 prepared scallops or queens with their corals
16 raw peeled tiger prawns
450 g (1 lb) monkfish fillet, cut into 2.5 cm
  (1 in) cubes
3 tablespoons olive oil
2 tablespoons lemon juice
2 tablespoons chopped fresh chervil or parsley
salt and freshly ground black pepper
1 small orange, halved and thinly sliced
1 lemon, thinly sliced
1 lime, thinly sliced

8 x 25 cm (10 in) fine metal skewers

Mix the oil, lemon juice, chopped chervil or parsley and some salt and pepper together in a large bowl.
Add the scallops, prawns and monkfish and mix together well.
Cover and leave to marinate at room temperature for 30 minutes or for up to 2 hours in the fridge.
Thread the scallops, prawns and monkfish on to the skewers, alternating them with folded slices of orange, lemon and lime.
Barbecue the kebabs over medium-hot coals for 8–10 minutes, turning and basting with the leftover marinade now and then.

Hua Hin Beach Red Snapper

I cooked this at Hua Hin on the beach of the head-shaped stones to the delight of many local fishermen and their families. It's an experience they, and I, will never forget. Just wait 'til you taste it. Substitute red snapper with grey snapper, salmon, trout or sea bass if you wish.

Serves 4
4 x 350 g (12 oz) red snapper
4 heaped tablespoons Thai red curry paste
4 heaped tablespoons coconut milk powder
4 limes
4 garlic cloves, peeled
4 spring onions

banana leaves or extra thick foil and cocktail sticks soaked in cold water for 30 minutes

Clean the snapper, remove the scales by scraping them from the tail end to the head with a large blunt knife and then cut off the fins. Cut several deep slashes into both sides of each fish and place them in the centre of a banana leaf or a large square of foil.

Mix the red curry paste and coconut milk powder together into a thick paste and rub it into the fish, making sure that some of it goes right down into the slashes.

Cut 2 of the limes into thin slices. Push one piece into each of the slashes along one side of each fish.

Thinly slice the garlic and spring onions and sprinkle over the top of each fish. Wrap the leaves or foil over the fish to make well-sealed parcels, secure with the cocktail sticks and barbecue over medium-hot coals for 15–20 minutes, turning occasionally, until the snappers are completely cooked through and tender.

Remove the cocktail sticks and serve each fish straight from its leaf or foil container. Allow each person to open their own parcel, as the aroma is sensational.

OPPOSITE Hua Hin Beach Red Snapper
BELOW An abundance of beautiful red onions and gorgeous white garlic. Chatachak Market, Bangkok.

VEGETARIAN DISHES

Fire-roasted Mediterranean Vegetables

These can be served as they are, warm straight from the barbecue, allowed to go cold and then lightly drizzled with a little lemon juice or balsamic vinegar for a salad, or turned into the most delicious picnic-style loaf (see opposite) for later on or the following day. Stunningly colourful, delightfully delicious.

Serves 4–6
2 red peppers
2 yellow peppers
1 medium aubergine, topped and tailed
3 small courgettes, topped and tailed
2 red onions, sliced into thick rounds
For the marinade:
2 garlic cloves, crushed
1 tablespoon chopped fresh basil
1 tablespoon chopped flatleaf parsley
250 ml (8 fl oz) olive oil
salt and freshly ground black pepper

Mix the ingredients for the marinade together in a large shallow dish.
Cut the peppers into quarters and remove the seeds. Cut the aubergine into 1 cm (½ in) thick rounds and cut the courgettes lengthways into slices.
Add the peppers, courgettes and onions to the dish, turn until well coated in the marinade and set aside for 1 hour if you wish.
At the last minute, toss the aubergines with the rest of the vegetables so that they don't absorb too much of the oil. Lift them on to the barbecue and cook over medium-hot coals for about 6–8 minutes, turning now and then and basting with any leftover marinade, until they are soft and richly coloured. Remove to a dish and sprinkle with a little more seasoning if you wish.

Fire-roasted Vegetable Loaf

Begin preparations for this the day before your barbecue. You can
add almost any flavours to this kind of loaf. Red or green pesto,
spinach, watercress and different cheeses would all work well
together with the grilled vegetables.

1 quantity roasted vegetables (see opposite)
1 rustic round loaf measuring about 25 cm (10 in) across
3–4 tablespoons tapenade (black olive paste)
50 g (2 oz) rocket leaves
225 g (8 oz) Mozzarella, very thinly sliced
1 small bunch of fresh basil, finely shredded
salt and freshly ground black pepper

Cut a 1 cm (½ in) slice off the top of the loaf. Hollow out the bread
with your fingers to leave a case with walls about 1 cm (½ in) thick.
Brush the inside of the case with a little of the leftover marinade and
then spread lightly with some of the tapenade. Line the inside of the
loaf with the rocket leaves.
As soon as the vegetables are cooked, remove them from the grill
and layer them up inside the loaf, sprinkling each layer with a little
shredded basil and seasoning – first the aubergine, then the sliced
Mozzarella, the red peppers, yellow peppers, onions and courgettes
and then finely spread over the remaining tapenade. The warmth of
the vegetables will slightly melt the cheese and wilt the rocket.
Replace the top of the loaf and wrap the whole thing in a sheet of
greaseproof paper and then a large sheet of clingfilm.
Put the loaf between 2 wooden boards and weight down – lots of
unopened cans will do the trick – and leave somewhere cool
overnight.
Unwrap the loaf and simply cut it into thick wedges to serve.

Marinated Goats' Cheese in Vine Leaf Parcels

This dish needs to be made with those small, individual goats' cheeses with a rind. Crotin de Chavignol is a name to look out for.

The vine leaves provide a protective coating, hold in all the marinade flavours and impart a lemony flavour to the cooked cheese. If you are lucky enough to be able to get hold of fresh vine leaves then great, but otherwise use vine leaves which have been vacuum-packed in brine, which are available from most delicatessens and larger supermarkets.

This dish is quite rich (the quantities below will make two small parcels per person) but do double the quantities if you don't think there's going to be enough for a main course.

Serves 4
8 large or 16 smaller vine leaves
4 x 100 g (4 oz) individual goats' cheeses
4 tablespoons olive oil
2 red finger chillies, seeded and finely chopped
2 teaspoons chopped fresh oregano
12 fresh basil leaves, finely shredded
1 garlic clove, finely chopped
½ teaspoon black peppercorns, coarsely crushed
8 small fresh bay leaves
coarse sea salt
Bruschetta-style Bread on page 150 to serve

cocktail sticks soaked in cold water for 30 minutes

If you are using fresh vine leaves, remove the tough part of the stem, drop them into a pan of lightly salted water and cook for about 4 minutes. Drain and refresh under cold water. If you are using preserved vine leaves, soak them in hot water, rinse in cold water and drain.

Cut the goats' cheeses in half horizontally into 2 smaller discs.

Mix the olive oil with the chopped chilli, oregano, basil, garlic, crushed pepper and a little salt.

Place a vine leaf on a plate (overlap 2 if they're quite small) and put a bay leaf and a little of the marinade into the centre.

Place a disc of goats' cheese on top, rind-side down, and then spoon over a bit more of the marinade, making sure that lots of the bits are covering the cut face of the cheese. Fold over the sides of the leaves and secure in place with one or more cocktail sticks. Repeat 3 more times.

Place the parcels in a shallow dish, pour over any oil left on the plate and set aside for 1 hour.

Brush the outside of the vine leaf parcels with a little more olive oil if necessary and barbecue over medium-hot coals for about 2½ minutes on each side.

Lift the parcels on to plates, remove the cocktail sticks and fold back the leaves. Serve with the Bruschetta-style Bread on page 150.

OPPOSITE Marinated Goats' Cheese in Vine Leaf Parcels

Aubergine Fold and Feta Rolls

These can either be served as a wonderful vegetarian main course or as an exciting side dish with any barbecued meats. The creamy, salty texture of the feta combined with the aubergine, sun-dried tomatoes, basil and a hint of garlic oil gets me salivating.

Serves 4
1 large aubergine, about 500 g (1¼ lb)
120 ml (4 fl oz) extra virgin olive oil
2 garlic cloves, crushed
finely grated zest of 1 lemon
1 small beef tomato
275 g (10 oz) Greek feta cheese
8 large fresh basil leaves
8 sundried tomatoes in olive oil, drained and finely sliced
salt and freshly ground black pepper

8 fine metal trussing skewers or cocktail sticks soaked in cold water for 30 minutes

Trim off the stalk end of the aubergine and then cut lengthways into 8 x 5 mm (¼ in) thick slices discarding the ends.
Arrange the slices in a single layer on a large baking tray, sprinkle lightly with some fine salt and set aside for 30 minutes to 1 hour – this will make them easier to roll later on as well as draw out some of the water.
Rinse the aubergines in cold water and then pat them really dry with kitchen paper.
Mix the olive oil with the garlic, lemon zest and some seasoning. Brush over both sides of each aubergine slice and then season with plenty of pepper. Place on the barbecue over medium-hot coals and barbecue for 2–3 minutes on each side until lightly charred. Set aside and leave to cool a little. Cut the tomato into 4 thick slices, discarding the ends and then cut each slice in half again to make 8 slices.
Cut the feta cheese into 8 slices. Place the aubergine slices on the work surface and place a piece of tomato in the middle of each slice. Arrange a slice of feta on top, then roughly tear the basil and scatter on top. Sprinkle over the sundried tomatoes and season with plenty of freshly ground black pepper. Flip over both ends to enclose the filling and secure with a cocktail stick.
Brush the outside of the rolls with the rest of the garlic and lemon oil and barbecue over medium-hot coals for 1–2 minutes on each side or until they are heated through and slightly golden. Serve at once.

Mexican Cheese Quesadillas

Who wants meat when you can have something that tastes this good?! 'Roll-up, roll-up, roll-up for a Que-sa-dillas', that's what you gonna do.

Serves 4
225 g (8 oz) Cheddar, coarsely grated
3–4 green chillies, seeded and finely chopped
4 tomatoes, skinned, seeded and diced
6 spring onions, trimmed and sliced
50 g (2 oz) pinenuts, toasted
4 tablespoons chopped fresh coriander
12 x 20 cm (8 in) soft flour tortillas

Mix the Cheddar with the chillies, diced tomatoes, spring onions, pinenuts and coriander.
Spoon some of the mixture in a line along one side of each tortilla and carefully roll them up.
Lay 3 rolls, side by side, in the centre of 4 large squares of extra-thick foil. Bring the sides together over the top and fold and pinch the edges together to make well-sealed parcels.
Rest the packets to the side of a medium-hot barbecue and cook for 10 minutes, turning frequently, until they have heated through and the cheese has melted. Unwrap and eat straight away.

Marinated Halloumi Cheese with Tang! Tang! Dressing

Halloumi is a waxy Cypriot cheese which will not melt during cooking which makes it perfect for slapping on the barbecue. It lacks flavour so it needs to be marinated first and then served with a fresh tangy dressing and lots of crunchy bread to mop up all the juices. 750 g (1½ lb) of cheese might seem like a lot but it is quite a dense, heavy cheese and it will give everyone 3 thin slices which is just about right for a main course.

Serves 4 as a main course or 8 as a starter
750 g (1½ lb) Halloumi, cut into 12 x 1 cm (½ in) thick slices
2 tablespoons olive oil
1 teaspoon balsamic vinegar
2 tablespoons lemon juice
1 tablespoon chopped fresh thyme
salt and freshly ground black pepper
For the Tang! Tang! dressing:
5 tablespoons extra virgin olive oil
4 plum tomatoes, skinned, seeded and diced
4 spring onions, trimmed and thinly sliced
½ small red onion, very finely chopped
2 tablespoons chopped fresh flatleaf parsley
1½ tablespoons balsamic vinegar
½ teaspoon crushed black peppercorns
50 g (2 oz) Calamata or other black olives to garnish

For the marinade, mix the oil, vinegar, lemon juice, thyme and some salt and pepper together in a large shallow dish. Add the slices of cheese, turn once or twice in the mixture and leave to marinate at room temperature for 1 hour.
Just before you are ready to cook the cheese, mix together all the ingredients for the dressing.
Lift the slices of cheese out of the marinade and barbecue in batches over medium-hot coals for 3 minutes or until they are golden, flipping them over with a fish slice half way through. Stir any leftover marinade into the dressing.
Place 3 slices of cheese on to each plate, spoon over the dressing and garnish with a few black olives. Serve with plenty of crusty fresh bread.

OPPOSITE Marinated Halloumi Cheese with Tang! Tang! Dressing

Spinach and Blue Cheese Mushroom Cups

Mushrooms release quite a lot of liquid when you cook them on a barbecue so the trick is to start them off gill-side down until they are almost tender. Then just flip them over and cover with a cooked topping which just needs to be heated through.

Serves 4
450 g (1 lb) fresh leaf spinach
3 tablespoons olive oil
1 garlic clove, crushed
1 tablespoon freshly squeezed lemon juice
8 evenly-sized large field mushrooms, wiped
2 tomatoes, thinly sliced
100 g (4 oz) Roquefort or Danish Blue, sliced
salt and freshly ground black pepper

Remove any large stalks from the spinach and wash it really well in plenty of cold water. Shake off the excess water (or give it a whizz in a salad spinner if you have one).
Heat 1 tablespoon of the olive oil in a large pan. Add the garlic and fry for a few seconds without letting it brown.
Add the spinach and stir-fry it over a high heat until it just wilts into the bottom of the pan. Add the lemon juice and some seasoning and toss together well.
Tip the spinach into a colander and press out the excess liquid. Transfer it to a board and roughly chop.
Remove the stalks from the mushrooms, brush both sides with a little olive oil and season well with some salt and pepper.
Barbecue the mushrooms gill-side down over medium-hot coals for 4 minutes. Slide to the front edge of the barbecue, flip them over and quickly top with the spinach, sliced tomatoes and blue cheese. Cook for another 4–5 minutes until the spinach is hot and the cheese has just started to melt. Eat straight away.

Korma Courgette and Chickpea Burgers

There's no reason why vegetarians should miss out on all the best barbecue-style dishes. These burgers are so good I bet even the meat-eaters will be envious! 'Who's gonna eat all the beefburgers then?'

Serves 4
1 onion, finely chopped
25 g (1 oz) butter
1 garlic clove, crushed
2 medium-sized courgettes, finely diced
225 g (8 oz) carrots, coarsely grated
397 g (14 oz) can chickpeas, drained and rinsed
75 g (3 oz) fresh wholemeal breadcrumbs
2 teaspoons mild or Korma curry paste
2 tablespoons crunchy peanut butter
1 medium egg yolk
3 tablespoons chopped fresh parsley
salt and freshly ground black pepper
To serve:
4 wholemeal or ciabatta bread rolls, halved
4 tablespoons mayonnaise
2 tablespoons chopped fresh coriander
a few crisp green salad leaves
2 tomatoes, thinly sliced

Fry the onion in the butter for 5 minutes until soft and lightly browned. Add the garlic, courgettes and carrots and fry for 5 minutes over a high heat until soft. Leave to cool.
Blend the chickpeas in a food processor until smooth. Scrape them into a bowl and mix in the cooked vegetables and the remaining ingredients.
Shape the mixture into 4 x 10 cm (4 in) flat discs, either by hand or by pressing the mixture into a metal pastry cutter. Cover and chill for at least 2 hours or until required.
Brush the outside of each burger with a little oil and barbecue over medium-hot coals for 6–7 minutes on each side.
Lightly toast the bread rolls, cut-side down, on the barbecue for a couple of minutes. Mix the mayonnaise with the coriander and spread a little over the bottom half of each bun. Cover with the salad leaves, sit a burger on top and finish with a few slices of tomato and the rest of the mayonnaise.

Chargrilled Asparagus and Spring Onion Bruschetta with Parmesan Flakes

The flavour of both these long slender vegetables is amazingly enhanced when cooked on a barbecue and they are beautifully complemented by the saltiness of the cheese. These would also make a nice starter for a special three-course barbecue 'meal'.

Serves 4
450 g (1 lb) asparagus
2 bunches (about 16) spring onions
juice of ½ lemon
3 tablespoons olive oil
2 garlic cloves, chopped
50 g (2 oz) Parmesan
1 loaf of ciabatta
1 garlic clove, peeled but left whole
salt and freshly ground black pepper

Trim the asparagus and spring onions and place in a shallow dish with the lemon juice, olive oil, chopped garlic and some seasoning. Leave them to marinate for 15 minutes. Peel thin shavings off the piece of Parmesan with a sharp potato peeler and set aside on a plate ready for sprinkling later.

Cut the ciabatta in half lengthways like you would a bread roll and then across into 4. Lightly toast the pieces over the barbecue or under the grill for a couple of minutes until golden. Remove, rub the cut side of each slice with the whole garlic clove and set aside on 4 plates.

Lift the asparagus out of the marinade and barbecue over medium-hot coals for about 2–3 minutes, turning now and then. Now add the spring onions to the rack and continue to cook both vegetables for a further 3–4 minutes, until they are tender and lightly browned on all sides.

Divide the spring onions and asparagus between the prepared brushcetta, spoon over a little more of the garlic and lemon oil and season with a little salt and pepper. Sprinkle the tops with the Parmesan shavings and eat straight away while the vegetables are still warm.

OPPOSITE Chargrilled Asparagus and Spring Onion Bruschetta with Parmesan Flakes
BELOW Jammin' with 'The Coyabalites'. Check out the shirts. Port Antonio, Jamaica.

Jammin' Baked Pumpkin with Vegetable and Coconut Curry

I made this on the street in Port Antonio, Jamaica. The band was playing, I started swaying and the barbecue was glowing white. There they would probably use things such as green mangoes and papaya, aubergines, christophenes, taro, yams and plantains in the curry – so if you have an Afro-Caribbean grocer nearby, simply substitute the vegetables below with whichever ones take your fancy. It is quite mild but you can adjust the amount of red chilli to suit your taste if you wish. P.S. Don't forget the music.

Serves 4
1 small pumpkin or acorn squash, weighing about 2 kg (4½ lb)
2 tablespoons vegetable oil
1 large onion, chopped
2 garlic cloves, crushed
2.5 cm (1 in) fresh root ginger, peeled and finely grated
2 red chillies, seeded and finely chopped
2 tablespoons medium curry powder
6 whole cloves
2 fresh bay leaves
450 g (1 lb) sweet potato, peeled and cut into 2.5 cm (1 in) chunks
1 large red pepper, seeded and cut into 2.5 cm (1 in) chunks
1 small aubergine, cut into 2.5 cm (1 in) chunks
450 ml (15 fl oz) vegetable stock
397 g (14 oz) can black-eyed peas, red kidney beans or pigeon peas (gungo peas), drained and rinsed
400 g (14 oz) can coconut milk
50 g (2 oz) callaloo or fresh spinach, washed and large stalks removed
salt and freshly ground black pepper

Trim the stalk from the pumpkin so that it can stand upright. Then take a 5 cm (2 in) slice off the top and scoop out the seeds and the fibrous part with a spoon and discard.

Season the inside of the pumpkin really well and then replace the lid and wrap in 2 large, oiled sheets of extra thick foil.

Nestle it into the embers of a medium-hot barbecue and cook for 45 minutes to 1 hour, turning it frequently. After 30 minutes go easy as you turn it, as it will have become tender and you don't want it to break. The skin will be quite dark at the end of cooking, but don't worry, this is how it should be.

Meanwhile for the curry, heat the oil in a large saucepan. Add the onion and fry for 5 minutes until soft.

Add the garlic, ginger and chillies and fry for 1 minute. Add the curry powder, cloves and bay leaves and fry for a further minute.

Add the sweet potato, red pepper and aubergine, stir in the stock and bring everything up to a gentle simmer. Cover and cook gently for 15 minutes.

Add the black eyed peas and the coconut milk and simmer for another 5–10 minutes until everything is tender.

Stir in the callaloo or spinach and cook for 1–2 minutes until it has wilted down into the sauce. Season well with some salt and pepper.

Remove the pumpkin from the fire and carefully unwrap it. Lift off the lid, spoon in the curry and replace the lid if you wish. Serve straight away with any leftover curry and plenty of cooked rice or warmed roti-style bread. Keep that music playing.

Whole Grilled Aubergines with Tricolour Stuffing

Aubergines are probably one of the most versatile and successful vegetables that you can cook on the barbecue. Here, whole ones have been partly cooked and then stuffed with a rich tomato and herb sauce. You could finish them off with some grated cheese at the end if you wish.

Serves 4
4 x 225 g (8 oz) long, slim aubergines
5 tablespoons olive oil
2 onions, finely chopped
3 garlic cloves, crushed
6 plum tomatoes or 397 g (14 oz) can premium
   plum tomatoes, roughly chopped
2 tablespoons tomato purée
3 tablespoons chopped fresh flatleaf parsley
juice of ½ lemon
salt and freshly ground black pepper
Garlic Pitta Fingers on page 150 to serve

Rub a little oil over the outside of the aubergines and pierce near the stem ends with a fork so that they don't pop off during cooking. Barbecue over medium-hot coals for 10–12 minutes, turning them now and then, until lightly browned. Remove and leave to cool slightly.

Meanwhile heat the rest of the oil (there should be about 3 tablespoons) in a frying pan. Add the onion and garlic and fry gently for 6–7 minutes until soft but not browned.

Add the tomatoes and the tomato purée, increase the heat and simmer quite vigorously for 4–5 minutes until reduced to a thick sauce. Stir in the parsley and lemon juice and season well with salt and pepper.

Make a deep slit lengthways into each aubergine and open them up into a pocket. Spoon in the tomato sauce, place each one into the centre of a 46 cm (18 in) square of extra-thick foil and pinch the edges together to make a well-sealed parcel.

Return the parcels to the barbecue and cook for a further 14–16 minutes until tender. Unwrap and serve with the garlic pitta bread.

VARIATION

If you wish, 5 minutes before the aubergines are ready, open up the foil parcels and fold back the foil slightly. Sprinkle the tomato stuffing with a little crumbled cheese (soft yoghurt cheese, feta, Kefalotiri, Halloumi or Cheddar) and finish cooking until the cheese has melted. Naughty... but very nice.

VEGETABLES, SIDE DISHES, & BREADS

BARBECUE VEGETABLES

Oriental Mixed Vegetable Parcels

Pop these little packets to the side of the rack and serve them with anything with a faintly oriental flavour. You could also serve them with some steamed rice for a light vegetarian main course.

Serves 4
450 g (1 lb) mixed mushrooms such as shiitake, chestnut, oyster and small field mushrooms
8 spring onions, trimmed
100 g (4 oz) fresh beansprouts
4 tablespoons light soy sauce
2 tablespoons dry sherry
2 tablespoons sunflower oil
1 teaspoon clear honey
5 cm (2 in) fresh root ginger, peeled and finely chopped
2 garlic cloves, finely chopped
4 green cardamom pods, cracked

Wipe the mushrooms and thickly slice. Cut each spring onion into 2.5 cm (1 in) lengths.
Pile the mushrooms, spring onions and beansprouts into the centre of four 30 cm (12 in) squares of extra-thick foil and then bring the sides of the foil up around the sides of the vegetables.
Mix the soy sauce with the rest of the ingredients. Divide the mixture equally between the parcels and then pleat the edges of the foil together to seal.
Cook the parcels to the side of the barbecue over medium-hot coals for 8 minutes until the vegetables are tender. These would go wonderfully with the Chinese Lattice Pork on page 67.

Char-roasted New Potato Skewers

Everyone knows that you can finish off baked potatoes on a barbecue, but you can also do new potatoes too, simply threaded on to skewers first. They become nicely roasted on the outside and make a great side dish to any barbecued meats or fish such as Sally's Salmon Steaks on page 100.

Serves 4
750 g (1½ lb) new potatoes, scrubbed
4 tablespoons olive oil
coarse sea salt and freshly ground black pepper

8 x 15 cm (6 in) bamboo skewers soaked in cold water for 30 minutes

Cook the potatoes in boiling salted water for about 12–15 minutes or until almost tender.
Drain them well and then tip them back into the pan and add the oil, salt and black pepper. Toss together well.
Thread 4 potatoes on to each skewer and barbecue over medium-hot coals for 7–8 minutes, turning regularly, until golden.

VARIATION
Stretch 16 rashers of rindless streaky bacon with the back of a knife and then cut each one in half. Wrap a piece of bacon around each potato, thread on to skewers and cook as above.

Salt 'n' Pepper Fire-baked Tatties

Whole potatoes are really almost impossible to cook fully on a barbecue, firstly because the skins tend to get too black before the insides are done, and secondly they would need about 1½ hours and most charcoal barbecues don't stay hot for that long. I always start mine off in the oven and then nestle them in amongst the coals to crisp up and finish cooking. Alternatively, cook them in the microwave for about 8–10 minutes before finishing on the coals.

Serves 4

4 x 275g (10 oz) baking potatoes or sweet
   potatoes
2 tablespoons olive oil
1 teaspoon coarse sea salt
1 teaspoon freshly ground black pepper

Scrub the potatoes if necessary, dry well and bake in the oven at 200°C/400°F/Gas mark 6 for about 40 minutes until almost tender.

Rub the outside of the potatoes with plenty of olive oil, sprinkle on all sides with plenty of salt and pepper – about ¼ teaspoon of each – and then wrap each one tightly in a triple-thickness square of extra-thick foil.

Push the potatoes in amongst the coals of a medium-hot barbecue and cook for another 30–40 minutes, turning frequently so that they cook evenly and don't burn, until they are cooked all the way through and the skins are crispy.

Unwrap the potatoes, cut them open and serve with plenty of butter, one of the savoury butters on pages 31–2, soured cream and chives, some grated cheese or spicy baked beans.

Sweet Grilled Onions with Balsamic Splash

Onions are a bit tricky to cook on a barbecue because they are quite dense, and they tend to brown too much before they are really tender. I've found that the trick is to partly cook them first and here I've simmered them in a little sugar syrup to enhance their sweetness and help them to caramelize even more. The mild acidity of the balsamic vinegar helps to cut through the sweetness and the combination of the two flavours is heaven.

Serves 4

4 large onions, unpeeled
2 tablespoons granulated sugar
120 ml (4 fl oz) water
salt and freshly ground black pepper
a few dashes of balsamic vinegar and olive oil to
   serve

4 x 18–25 cm (6–8 in) flat metal skewers (they
   need to fit into your largest frying pan or shallow
   casserole dish)

Quarter the onions leaving the root end intact and then pull off the layers of skin. The wedges will stay together in one piece.

Put the sugar and water into a large, deep frying pan or shallow casserole dish and leave it over a low heat until the sugar has dissolved. Bring the mixture to the boil and boil for 2 minutes.

Meanwhile thread a skewer diagonally from the root end of each onion wedge up through the onion to the point. This will help to keep them in shape during cooking.

Lower the onion skewers into the sugar syrup, cover and simmer for 7–8 minutes until softened. Carefully lift out on to a plate and set aside until you are ready to finish them on the barbecue.

Barbecue the onions over medium-hot coals for 5 minutes, turning and brushing them with the leftover sugar syrup, until they are richly browned.

Transfer them to a serving plate and pull out the skewers. Sprinkle with a little salt and pepper, add a splash of balsamic vinegar and a little olive oil and serve hot.

Husky Jacket Corn on the Cob with Chilli and Spring Onion Dressing

Sweetcorn cooked on a barbecue in their husks become really tender because they almost steam in their own juices. The trick is to soak them in cold water for at least 1 hour beforehand so that the husks don't catch fire during cooking. They're flaming lovely!

Serves 4–6
4–6 ears of sweetcorn in their husks
175 g (6 oz) butter
4 teaspoons chilli oil (or more if you dare)
4 green chillies, seeded and very finely chopped
4 spring onions, trimmed and thinly sliced
2 teaspoons lemon or lime juice
salt and freshly ground black pepper

Soak the sweetcorn in cold water for at least 1 hour.
Remove the corn from the water, drain away the excess and barbecue them over medium-hot coals for 30 minutes, turning them every now and then.
Meanwhile, put the butter into a pan and leave over a low heat until melted. Spoon any scum off the surface and then pour the clear butter into a bowl, leaving behind the milky white liquid.
Just before the sweetcorn is ready, heat the chilli oil in a small clean pan, add the green chillies and fry for 1 minute. Remove from the heat and add the clarified butter, spring onions, lemon juice and plenty of seasoning.
Pull away the browned husks from the outside of the corn, transfer the ears on to plates and spoon over the warm dressing. Eat with plenty of crusty bread to mop up all the juices.

LEFT Back to basics – inside an Arawak cave at Duncan's.
Near Montego Bay, Jamaica.
OPPOSITE Husky Jacket Corn on the Cob with Chilli and
Spring Onion Dressing

Chunky Caramelized Shallot Chutney

Cooked like this, in one large foil parcel, these shallots almost turn into a sweet onion-style chutney. Cut a deep cross in the top of them if they're quite large to help them cook through more quickly and soak up all those lovely flavours.

Serves 4
450 g (1 lb) shallots
4 fresh bay leaves
2 tablespoons demerara sugar
25 g (1 oz) butter
salt and freshly ground black pepper

Peel the shallots and pile them with bay leaves into the centre of one large square of extra-thick foil. Pleat the edges together over the top and then fold up the sides to make a well-sealed parcel.
Place the parcel to the side of a medium-hot barbecue and cook for 30 minutes until the shallots are soft.
Carefully open up the parcel and sprinkle them with the brown sugar. Stir them around a little, dot here and there with the butter, season with salt and pepper and reseal them.
Return the parcel to the barbecue for another 10 minutes during which time the sugar and the butter will caramelize them to a rich golden brown. Serve them while they are still hot with any barbecued meats.

Cumin-crusted Butternut Squash

In the townships of Cape Town, South Africa, it seems that everyone goes to the butcher, buys their meat, then steps out the back and cooks it free of charge on the butchers glowing barbecue in a warm, friendly, taverna-style manner. You might say it's a 'buy and braii' shop (braii means barbecue in South Africa). I wanted to give them a veggie alternative and the wonderful aroma emanating from the coals got them all buzzing, especially when they tasted them.

Serves 4
1 large or 2 small butternut squash
2 garlic cloves, crushed
2 teaspoons ground cumin
2–3 tablespoons olive oil
½ lemon
salt and freshly ground black pepper

Cut the butternut squash in half and scoop out all the fibres and seeds. Cut each half into 3 wedges and make shallow criss-cross cuts into the flesh of each piece with a small, sharp knife.
Put the crushed garlic, cumin, olive oil, a good squeeze of lemon juice and some salt and pepper into a bowl and mix together well.
Rub the mixture over the fleshy side of each wedge of squash and cook over medium-hot coals for 2–3 minutes on each side, until lightly browned.
Now flip the pieces over on to their backs and cook skin-side down for a further 6–8 minutes, basting every now and then with any leftover cumin mixture, until the flesh is tender when you pierce it with a skewer. Serve at once.

Sweet and Sour Minted Aubergines

This dish would go really well with some plainly barbecued chicken or lamb so that the fresh minty flavour of the sauce doesn't get too lost. It can be made with long slender aubergines, cut diagonally across into oval-shaped slices or those baby, egg-shaped ones which will just need to split in half lengthways.

Serves 4
450 g (1 lb) aubergines, topped and tailed
6 garlic cloves, very finely chopped
5 tablespoons olive oil
175 ml (6 fl oz) white wine vinegar
4 tablespoons caster sugar
salt and freshly ground black pepper
6 tablespoons chopped fresh mint

Gently fry the garlic in 1 tablespoon of the olive oil for 1–2 minutes to cook out the raw garlic flavour, but do not let it brown.
Add the vinegar and sugar to the pan and cook over a low heat until the sugar has completely dissolved.
Bring the syrup to the boil and boil for 7–8 minutes until it has reduced by half. Set to one side.
Cut the aubergines into 1 cm (½ in) thick slices if large and in half lengthways if small. Brush both sides generously with the remaining olive oil, season well with salt and pepper and barbecue over medium-hot coals for about 5 minutes on each side until browned and tender.
Transfer the aubergines to a shallow serving dish. Stir the mint into the sauce, spoon over the aubergines and serve glowingly hot or chillingly cold. Either way, they're delicious.

OPPOSITE Sweet and Sour Minted Aubergines

Buttered Chargrilled Sweetcorn

This is an alternative way of cooking sweetcorn. It is started off in a foil parcel until it is tender and then unwrapped and finished off over the coals so that it chars and takes on a lovely smoky flavour. I think this is nicest served with just plain butter so that you don't mask that special smoky flavour.

Serves 6
6 ears of sweetcorn, peeled
1 tablespoon vegetable oil
25 g (1 oz) butter
salt and freshly ground black pepper

Rub the sweetcorn with a little oil, dot here and there with the butter, season well with salt and pepper and wrap up tightly in foil.
Barbecue over medium-hot coals for 20 minutes, turning now and then, to ensure that they cook evenly.
Unwrap the corn, return them to the barbecue and cook directly over the coals for about another 15 minutes, turning now and then, until richly coloured. Sprinkle with a little more salt and pepper and serve with some extra butter.

Best Barbecue Boulangère Potatoes

If you can make these in the oven I thought, then there's no reason why you can't do them on the barbecue – and I was right. They make a great potato side dish to any cooked meat, but lamb is extra good.

Serves 4
750 g (1½ lb) floury potatoes such as King
    Edwards, peeled
1 medium onion, halved and sliced
2 garlic cloves, finely chopped
300 ml (10 fl oz) chicken or vegetable stock
2 teaspoons fresh thyme leaves
40 g (1½ oz) butter
salt and freshly ground black pepper

Slice the potatoes thinly and pile them into the centre of 4 x 30 cm (12 in) squares of foil. Bring the foil up around the side of the potatoes and divide the onion, garlic, chicken stock and thyme between each one.
Season the potatoes with salt and pepper, dot here and there with the butter and scrunch the edges of the foil together well to seal.
Place the parcels to the side of the barbecue and cook for 15–20 minutes, moving them around now and then to make sure they cook evenly. At the end of the cooking time the potatoes will have absorbed all the stock and butter and become tender.

Chargrilled Sweet Potatoes, Pumpkin and Parsnips

All these vegetables have a naturally high sugar content so they cook beautifully over the barbecue, where the sugar naturally caramelizes and browns. I have served them with a chilli and lime butter but you could also turn them into a wonderful main meal salad by adding some cooked chicken and blue cheese (see the Variation that follows).

Serves 4–6

2 large sweet potatoes, peeled
450 g (1 lb) pumpkin or squash, peeled and any
   seeds removed
4 large parsnips, trimmed
4 large carrots, trimmed
6 tablespoons olive oil
coarse sea salt and freshly ground black pepper
For the chilli and lime butter:
100 g (4 oz) slightly salted butter, softened
2 red chillies, seeded and finely chopped
a good pinch of cayenne pepper
finely grated zest of 1 lime
1–2 teaspoons lime juice
2 tablespoons chopped fresh coriander

Cut the potatoes and pumpkin into 1 cm (½ in) thick slices. Halve the parsnips and carrots lengthways.
Cook all the vegetables separately in boiling salted water for 5–10 minutes until just tender. Drain well and dry on kitchen paper. They can now be set aside at this stage until you are ready to cook if you wish.
For the chilli and lime butter, simply beat all the ingredients together in a bowl until well combined. Spoon on to a sheet of clingfilm or non-stick baking parchment, shape into a thin roll and leave in the fridge or freezer until firm or until required.

Brush the vegetables on both sides with plenty of oil and season well with salt and pepper. Barbecue over medium-hot coals for 4–6 minutes on each side until lightly browned.
Remove the chilli and lime butter from the fridge and cut it into thin slices. Lift the cooked vegetables on to a large serving plate, dot with the butter slices and leave until melted before serving.

VARIATION
Chicken, Blue Cheese and Grilled Vegetable Salad

Serves 6

Cook the vegetables as above and leave to go cold. Then cut them into small chunky pieces.
Mix 4 tablespoons of sunflower oil with 1 teaspoon of finely grated orange zest, 4 tablespoons each of freshly squeezed orange and lemon juice, 1 tablespoon of finely chopped fresh rosemary and some salt and pepper.
Brush a little of the mixture over 4 boned chicken breasts and barbecue over medium-hot coals for 5–6 minutes on each side. Leave to go cold and then cut across into thin slices.
Put the barbecued vegetables and chicken into a large salad bowl and toss in the rest of the orange and rosemary dressing.
Sprinkle the top with 175 g (6 oz) of crumbled Dolcelatte and serve with maybe a crisp watercress and baby spinach leaf salad.

Marvellous Mediterranean Fire Tomatoes

Try to look out for large beefsteak tomatoes with lots of flavour. The 'marmande' variety from Provence, France and Morocco are absolutely superb and you do occasionally see them during the summer months.

Serves 6
6 firm beefsteak tomatoes
4 tablespoons olive oil
4 garlic cloves, finely chopped
1 tablespoon chopped fresh oregano or marjoram
salt and freshly ground black pepper
12 pitted black olives, finely chopped

Cut the tomatoes in half and place rounded-side down in a shallow dish.
Sprinkle each one with some olive oil, garlic, oregano or marjoram, salt and pepper and set aside for 1 hour or until you are ready to finish them on the barbecue.
Sprinkle the tomatoes with the chopped olives, lift them on to the side of the barbecue and cook, rounded-side down only, for about 10–12 minutes until tender.

OPPOSITE Marvellous Mediterranean Fire Tomatoes
BELOW Chargrilled Sweet Potatoes (see page 135)

SALADS & SIDE DISHES

Nice Rice Noodle Doodle Salad

Rice noodles, or 'stir-fry noodles' as they are sometimes called, cook or rather soak in a matter of minutes. They are very light and easy to eat and would be a great accompaniment to anything with a Far Eastern flavour.

Serves 6–8
175 g (6 oz) rice vermicelli noodles
juice of 2 limes
2 small garlic cloves, very finely chopped
8 spring onions, trimmed and thinly sliced
2 red chillies, seeded and very finely chopped
2 limes
1 tablespoon groundnut or sunflower oil
4 teaspoons sesame oil
3 tablespoons Thai fish sauce
3 tablespoons chopped fresh coriander

Drop the noodles into a large pan of boiling salted water. Take the pan off the heat and leave them to soak for 3 minutes.
Drain the noodles well, tip them into a salad bowl and leave to go cold.
Finely grate the zest from 1 lime and squeeze out the juice from both. Add to the noodles with the rest of the ingredients just before serving and toss together lightly.

Tangier Mint Tabbouleh

This is the classic Middle Eastern salad made with cracked wheat, also known as bulghar or burghul wheat. You'll find it in health food shops or usually alongside the dried pulses and beans in the supermarket. It's so colourful and goes with all types of barbecued food.

Serves 6–8
175 g (6 oz) cracked wheat
½ cucumber
4 salad tomatoes, skinned, seeded and diced
1 small red onion, finely chopped
3 tablespoons chopped fresh mint
3 tablespoons chopped fresh parsley
1½ tablespoons Best Ever Mustard French
   Dressing (see page 30)
2 tablespoons extra virgin olive oil
3 tablespoons freshly squeezed lemon juice
salt and freshly ground black pepper

Put the cracked wheat into a bowl and cover it with lots of boiling water. Leave it to soak for 25 minutes.
Tip the cracked wheat into a sieve and leave it to drain really well. Then spoon it into the centre of a large clean tea towel and squeeze out all the excess moisture. This is really important or you will end with a very soggy salad.
Cut the cucumber into small dice. Transfer the cracked wheat to a serving bowl and stir in the cucumber, tomatoes, red onion, chopped mint, chopped parsley, French dressing, olive oil, lemon juice and some seasoning. Stir together well and serve.

Caribbean Mixed Bean and Cashew Nut Salad

Beans go down a treat in Jamaica and the other Caribbean islands, so serve this up with some of their other specialities for an authentic West Indian feast.

Serves 8
397 g (14 oz) can butter beans
397 g (14 oz) can black-eyed peas or red kidney beans
350 g (12 oz) can sweetcorn kernels
3 celery sticks, sliced
1 red pepper, seeded and chopped
6 spring onions, trimmed and sliced
100 g (4 oz) cashew nuts, roasted
2 tablespoons mayonnaise
2 tablespoons soured cream
1 garlic clove, crushed (optional)
1 tablespoon lemon juice
salt and freshly ground black pepper

Tip the canned beans into a large sieve and rinse off the starchy liquid with cold water. Drain well and then tip them into a large salad bowl.
Drain the sweetcorn and add to the bowl with the celery, red pepper, spring onions, roasted cashew nuts, mayonnaise, soured cream, garlic and lemon juice. Season with a little salt and pepper to taste and serve.

Ainsley's Ultimate Creole Cabbage Salad

For a great alternative to your usual coleslaw this salad really hits the crunch spot, and gives your tastebuds a delightfully creamy, cool, spicy kick.

Serves 6–8
275 g (10 oz) white cabbage, cored and very thinly shredded
2 celery sticks, thinly sliced
1 green pepper, seeded and very thinly sliced
4 spring onions, trimmed and thinly sliced
½ tablespoon Dijon mustard
1 teaspoon creamed horseradish
½ teaspoon Tabasco sauce
1 tablespoon red wine vinegar
2 tablespoons olive oil
2 tablespoons mayonnaise
2 tablespoons chopped fresh dill
pinch of cayenne pepper
salt and freshly ground black pepper

Mix the cabbage, celery, green pepper and spring onions together in a large bowl.
Mix the mustard, creamed horseradish, Tabasco sauce and vinegar in a small bowl and then gradually whisk in the oil. Stir in the mayonnaise and season well with salt and pepper.
Stir the dressing and chopped dill into the vegetables just before serving so that the cabbage stays nice and crunchy.

Cor! Puy Lentil, Red Onion and Sundried Tomato Salad

Make this salad a little while before you need it so that all the flavours have time to soak into the lentils. Puy lentils have a greeny, slate-grey colour and definitely the best flavour. If your local supermarket doesn't have any, you should have more luck in a health food shop. Or, if all else fails and you're in a hurry, use tinned green lentils which require no cooking.

Serves 8

225 g (8 oz) Puy lentils, picked over for stones
1 fresh bay leaf
1 teaspoon red wine vinegar
2 garlic cloves, peeled and left whole
pinch of caster sugar
1 large red onion, finely chopped
50 g (2 oz) sundried tomatoes in oil, drained and chopped
1–2 tablespoons balsamic vinegar (depending on your taste)
4 tablespoons extra virgin olive oil
100 g (4 oz) goats' cheese or feta cheese, crumbled
3 tablespoons chopped fresh flatleaf parsley
salt and freshly ground black pepper

Put the lentils into a pan with the bay leaf, vinegar, 1 whole garlic clove, sugar and a little salt and pepper. Cover with 1.2 litres (2 pints) of cold water, bring to the boil and leave to simmer for about 25 minutes until just tender but still holding their shape.

Drain the lentils well, discarding the bay leaf and whole garlic clove. Tip them into a salad bowl and leave to go cold.

Finely chop the remaining garlic clove and stir it into the lentils with the rest of the ingredients. Season to taste with salt and pepper and chill for 2 hours before serving.

OPPOSITE Cor! Puy Lentil, Red Onion and Sundried Tomato Salad
BELOW I wonder how Arsenal are doing? Hua Hin Beach, Thailand.

Creamy Crisp Green Salad with Guacamole Dressing

This makes a nice change from the usual leafy salads and would be ideal if you were throwing a Mexican themed barbecue. It is essential that you use very crisp, robust lettuce leaves for this so that they can hold up under the weight of the rich, creamy dressing.

Serves 8

2 cos, Romaine or Webbs lettuce (or a mixture)
75 g (3 oz) prepared watercress, broken into
   sprigs
4 slices medium-sliced white bread
sunflower oil for deep-frying
For the guacamole dressing:
1 ripe avocado
1 teaspoon Dijon mustard
2 tablespoons lemon juice
a good dash of Tabasco sauce
65 ml (2½ fl oz) sunflower oil
salt and freshly ground black pepper

Break the lettuce into small pieces and toss in a large salad bowl with the watercress sprigs. Set aside in the fridge to chill while you make the croûtons and the dressing.
Heat 2.5 cm (1 in) of oil in a large a pan to 190°C/375°F. Remove and discard the crusts from the slices of bread and cut it into 1 cm (½ in) cubes.
Deep-fry the cubes of bread for 1 minute until golden. Lift out with a slotted spoon on to kitchen paper and leave to drain and cool.
For the dressing, halve the avocado, remove the stone and scoop the flesh into a food processor. Add the mustard, lemon juice, Tabasco sauce and some salt and pepper and blend until smooth.
With the motor still running, gradually pour in the oil in a slow steady stream. It will gradually become thick and creamy.
Just before serving, spoon the dressing over the chilled salad leaves, sprinkle with the croûtons and some seasoning and toss together lightly.

VARIATION

For an alternative Creamy Garlic Dressing, whisk 1 crushed garlic clove, 2 tablespoons of lemon juice, ½ teaspoon of Dijon mustard, 1 medium egg yolk and plenty of salt and pepper together in a small bowl. Gradually whisk in 150 ml (5 fl oz) of olive oil. Toss with the salad leaves and sprinkle with some Parmesan shavings if you wish.

New Potato Salad with Gherkins, Chives and Soured Cream

A barbecue wouldn't be complete without a potato salad, and although there are a hundred and one things you can add to the potatoes, I still like the taste of soured cream and chives the best. It's classically cool...

Serves 8

900 g (2 lb) waxy new potatoes such as Jersey
   Royals, scrubbed
3 tablespoons Best Ever Mustard French Dressing
   (see page 30)
175 g (6 oz) small pickled cucumbers, sliced
1 small onion, finely chopped
65 ml (2½ fl oz) soured cream
65 ml (2½ fl oz) mayonnaise
4 tablespoons snipped fresh chives
salt and freshly ground black pepper

Cook the potatoes in boiling salted water for 15–20 minutes until just tender. Drain them well and then cut in half or into quarters if quite large.
Tip the potatoes into a serving bowl, stir in the mustard French dressing and set aside until cold. Chill in the fridge until just before you are ready to serve.
Add the pickled cucumbers and chopped onion to the potatoes and gently mix together. Mix the soured cream, mayonnaise and chives together, stir into the potatoes and season to taste with plenty of salt and pepper.

Fire-roasted Red Pepper and Nectarine Salad

Another simple salad that has the beautiful taste of chargrilled pepper, combined with nectarines infused with sweet-sharp balsamic vinegar, olly oil and pepper. There, now isn't that simple!

Serves 8
8 large red peppers
4 ripe but firm nectarines
4 teaspoons balsamic vinegar
6 tablespoons extra virgin olive oil
freshly ground black pepper

Cook the peppers on the barbecue or under the grill for about 20 minutes, turning them regularly, until the skins are completely blackened and blistered.

Drop them into a large plastic bag, seal in some air and leave until cool enough to handle. The captured steam helps to loosen the skins, making them easier to peel.

Cut the peppers in half, remove the skin and seeds and cut the flesh into long thin strips.

Place the peppers into a shallow dish with any juices. Halve the nectarines, remove the stones and thinly slice them into the dish with the peppers. Toss together gently.

Drizzle over the balsamic vinegar, olive oil and season with plenty of black pepper. Serve straight away.

Spicy Casablanca Couscous

'Out of all the places in the world you come to my barbecue.' This can either be served warm as a side dish or cold as a salad. Either way it is a delicious accompaniment to any grilled fish or meats. I'm sure Humphrey Bogart would have agreed.

Serves 6–8
3 tablespoons olive oil
1 garlic clove, very finely chopped
1 teaspoon ground cumin
1 teaspoon ground coriander
1 teaspoon paprika
350 ml (12 fl oz) chicken or vegetable stock
good pinch of saffron strands
6 spring onions, trimmed and thinly sliced
225 g (8 oz) couscous
2 red chillies, seeded and very finely chopped
50 g (2 oz) pinenuts, toasted
coarsely grated zest and juice of 1 lemon
1½ tablespoons chopped fresh coriander
1½ tablespoons chopped fresh mint
1½ tablespoons chopped fresh parsley

Heat 2 tablespoons of the oil in a large pan. Add the garlic, cumin, coriander and paprika and fry for 1 minute, stirring.

Add the stock and saffron and bring to the boil. Add the spring onions and then pour in the couscous in a steady steam and stir once.

Cover the pan with a tight-fitting lid, remove from the heat and set aside for 5 minutes to allow the grains to swell and absorb all the liquid.

If you are serving this warm, fork in the rest of the oil and the remaining ingredients now. Otherwise, leave the couscous to cool and chill in the fridge for 1 hour before adding all the other ingredients.

Cool Carrot, Cumin and Lemon Salad

A long list of ingredients is not always needed to make something that tastes absolutely scrumptious. This is a very simple salad which can be put together in not much more than five minutes. It would be great served with any barbecued foods, but will go exceptionally well with anything with a slightly spicy flavour.

Serves 6–8
750 g (1 lb) carrots
½ teaspoon salt
4 tablespoons sunflower oil
1 tablespoon cumin seeds
1 tablespoon black mustard seeds
4 teaspoons lemon juice

Top and tail and then peel the carrots. Either coarsely grate them or peel them lengthways with a potato peeler into long ribbons. Put the carrot into a bowl and toss with the salt.
Put the oil into a small pan. As soon as it is quite hot, toss in the cumin and mustard seeds and leave them to sizzle for a few seconds.
As soon as the mustard seeds begin to go off pop, pour the mixture over the carrots in the bowl and toss together with the lemon juice. That's it!

Peppy's Jamaican Rice and Peas

This is a very traditional Caribbean side dish and it's also regarded as the Jamaican coat of arms. The peas are either red kidney beans, pigeon peas or black-eyed peas, not the standard green variety. Most are available at the supermarket or in a Caribbean food shop, either dried or in cans. My Mum would cook this on most Sundays and all the children would be so impatient that half the pot was eaten before we sat down to eat. It's divinely delicious. Rub a little oil into your hands before chopping chillies – it protects the skin and makes it easy to wash off the heat from the seeds.

Serves 8
1 onion or 3 spring onions, finely chopped
1 tablespoon sunflower oil
25 g (1 oz) butter
2 garlic cloves, finely chopped
1 red finger chilli, seeded and very finely chopped
450 g (1 lb) long grain rice
2 sprigs of fresh thyme
7.5 cm (3 in) cinnamon stick (optional)
397 g (14 oz) can red kidney beans, black-eyed peas or pigeon peas
125 g (5 oz) creamed coconut, coarsely grated
1 litre (1¾ pints) hot water
salt and freshly ground black pepper

Fry the onion in the oil and butter for 2 minutes then add the garlic and chilli and fry for another 2 minutes over a medium heat.
Stir in the rice, thyme and cinnamon stick until everything is well coated in the oil.
Pour in the kidney beans, add the grated creamed coconut and stir until the coconut has dissolved so it's nice and creamy.
Then stir in the water with ½ teaspoon of salt, bring to the boil, cover and cook over a low heat for 25–30 minutes.
Remove from the heat and set aside, undisturbed, for 5 minutes.
Remove the thyme and cinnamon, season to taste with salt and pepper and serve.

OPPOSITE Peppy's Jamaican Rice and Peas

Minted Cucumber and Cherry Tom Tom Salad

This salad just sings out the word 'summer'. Served well chilled, it makes a light, refreshing side dish to any fish and meats.

Serves 6–8
2 cucumbers
450 g (1 lb) cherry tomatoes
4 tablespoons chopped fresh mint
2 tablespoons extra virgin olive oil
salt and freshly ground black pepper

Remove the peel of each cucumber in strips so that you give it a stripy look. Cut in half lengthways, scoop out the seeds with a teaspoon (or a melon baller does the job excellently) and slice it diagonally across into half-moon shaped pieces.
Place the cucumber in a colander, sprinkle with
1 teaspoon of salt and mix together well. Leave to drain for 1 hour.
Rinse off the salt under running cold water and dry it well on lots of kitchen paper or clean tea towels.
Halve the tomatoes and put them into a bowl with the cucumber, mint, olive oil and some ground black pepper.
Lightly stir together, cover and chill for 1 hour before serving.

Heavenly Hot Potato Salad with a Crispy Bacon Dressing

You must be sure to use firm maincrop potatoes for this dish so that they don't try to turn themselves into mash when you add the hot bacon dressing. Use a Wilja or Romano potato and don't stir them around too much once they're cooked.

Serves 6–8

1.5 kg (3 lb) firm potatoes
225 g (8 oz) rindless streaky bacon
1 onion, finely chopped
5 tablespoons sunflower oil
4 tablespoons cider vinegar
½ teaspoon English mustard powder
1½ teaspoons sugar
1 teaspoon celery seeds
1 teaspoon paprika
salt and freshly ground black pepper
2 tablespoons chopped fresh parsley

Peel the potatoes and cut them roughly into 2.5 cm (1½ in) chunks. Cook in boiling salted water for 15 minutes or until just tender.
Meanwhile, heat a large, dry frying pan over a high heat. Add the bacon (in batches if necessary) and fry for about 5 minutes on each side until crisp and richly golden.
Remove the bacon from the pan, leave to drain on kitchen paper and then crumble or chop it into small pieces.
Add the onion to the bacon fat left in the pan and fry for 5 minutes until soft. Add the oil, vinegar, mustard, sugar, celery seeds, paprika and seasoning and slowly bring the mixture to the boil. Leave to simmer gently for 5 minutes.
Drain the potatoes well, tip them into a large shallow dish and spoon over the hot dressing. Stir together very gently, add the bacon and the parsley and stir once more before serving.

BARBECUE BREADS

Here are a few ideas on what to do with ready-made breads and a recipe for a barbecue-baked bread too, cooked over the coals in a foil parcel.

The Best Traditional Garlic Butter Bread

Here is everyone's favourite and a few other variations. It is best to use long or thin, crusty breads such as French sticks or ciabatta so that the heat can get through to the middle and melt the butter before they burn on the outside.

Serves 6–8
1 long fat French stick
3 garlic cloves
75 g (3 oz) slightly salted butter, softened
3 tablespoons chopped fresh parsley
salt and freshly ground black pepper

Cut the bread diagonally into 2.5 cm (1 in) thick slices without cutting right through, keeping the loaf in shape as you go.
Peel the garlic, place it on a chopping board and lightly crush the cloves with the blade of a large knife. Sprinkle them with a little salt and continue to crush them using the side of the knife until they form a smooth paste.
Mix the butter with the garlic, parsley and some pepper.
Spread both sides of each slice of bread with a thin layer of the garlic butter and reassemble the loaf on one large or two smaller sheets of extra-thick foil.
Pleat the edges of the foil together well and leave the parcel on the side of the barbecue for 10–12 minutes, turning regularly, until crisp and hot.

VARIATIONS

Hot Herb and Sesame Bread Replace the French stick with a Parisienne or other long rustic French loaf. Omit the garlic and mix 2 tablespoons of chopped fresh dill, only 1 tablespoon of chopped fresh parsley, 3 thinly sliced spring onions, the finely grated rind and juice of ½ small lemon and 2 tablespoons of toasted sesame seeds into the butter.

Hot Cheese and Pesto Bread Replace the French stick with 2 loaves of ciabatta and use just 50 g (2 oz) of butter with 2 tablespoons of pesto, 2 tablespoons of chopped fresh basil and 15 g (½ oz) of finely grated Parmesan instead of the garlic and parsley.

Hot Foccacia 'Pizza' Bread Replace the French stick with 2 loaves of Italian herb foccacia, each cut into 10–12 wedges. Substitute 2 tablespoons of sundried tomato paste, 1 teaspoon of chopped fresh oregano and 2 tablespoons of finely chopped black olives for the garlic and parsley.

OPPOSITE, FROM LEFT TO RIGHT Hot Foccacia 'Pizza' Bread, The Best Traditional Garlic Butter Bread, Hot Herb and Sesame Bread and Hot Cheese and Pesto Bread

Garlic Pitta Fingers

These take a matter of minutes to make and they are so deliciously buttery and crunchy, be sure to make plenty of them. I can guarantee that they'll soon disappear! I melt the butter in the microwave, but be careful as it only takes seconds.

Serves 6
6 sesame or white pitta bread
50 g (2 oz) unsalted butter, melted
2 garlic cloves, very finely chopped
2 tablespoons chopped fresh parsley
salt and freshly ground black pepper

Place the butter in a small pan and heat gently until melted, add the garlic and parsley and just heat through. Set aside to allow the flavours to combine. Lightly slash the pittas on one side and place cut side up on to the rack on one side of the barbecue and cook for 1 minute until lightly toasted.
Turn the pittas over and spoon over the garlic butter. Cook for another 1–2 minutes, by which time the butter will be sizzling.
Lift the pitta bread on to a board, cut into thick fingers and serve whilst still crisp and warm.

Bruschetta-style Bread

This lightly toasted bread, scented with garlic and moistened with a little oil, goes superbly with any barbecued foods. Try to use large juicy cloves of fresh garlic and the best olive oil that you have to hand because it really will make all the difference. Also, if you leave out the garlic, and use an oil flavoured with perhaps fresh herbs or lemon, it will make a wonderful dessert with a selection of fresh cheeses and fruit.

Serves 4
1 loaf of ciabatta
1 garlic clove, halved
3–4 tablespoons olive oil

Cut the loaf of bread in half horizontally as if you were going to make a sandwich.
Lightly toast the bread on the barbecue for 1–2 minutes on each side. Remove it from the rack and quickly rub the cut face with the halved clove of garlic.
Drizzle over a little of the oil, cut it into chunky pieces and serve while still slightly warm.

Damper Beer Bread

This bread is made with beer but you could use all milk if you prefer. The texture of the finished bread is very similar to a scone and so it needs to be eaten as soon as it is made, preferably while it's still slightly warm.

Serves 6

225 g (8 oz) plain wholemeal flour

275 g (10 oz) self-raising flour plus 1 tablespoon for dusting

1 teaspoon salt

45 g (1½ oz) butter

175 ml (6 fl oz) light ale or bitter

175 ml (6 fl oz) milk

225 g (8 oz) mature Cheddar or Gruyère, coarsely grated

4 spring onions, trimmed and thinly sliced

cayenne pepper

Sift the flours and salt together into a bowl. Rub in the butter until the mixture looks like fine breadcrumbs.

Make a well in the centre, add the beer and milk and gradually mix together to make a soft dough.

Turn out on to a clean surface and knead briefly until smooth. Shape into a 25 cm (10 in) round and place in the centre of a large, double-thickness sheet of oiled extra-thick foil.

Score the top of the bread in a criss-cross pattern and sprinkle with 1 tablespoon of flour. Bring the edges of the foil together loosely over the top of the loaf and pleat together to seal.

Place the foil parcel on to the barbecue rack and cook over medium- hot coals for 10 minutes on each side.

Open the foil parcel and fold back the edges. Sprinkle the top of the loaf with the cheese, spring onions and cayenne pepper and leave for another 5 minutes until the cheese has melted. Remove from the foil and serve cut into thick wedges.

Me and Mum's
Rum Pu-Punch at
Blue Lagoon, Jamaica.
Still no sign of
Brooke Shields!

DESSERTS & DRINKS

BARBECUE DESSERTS

Here are a selection of delicious desserts which you can cook on the barbecue and a few which you can make in advance and have ready to hand when the cooking has come to an end.

Sydney Flambéed Fruits with Maple Syrup and Lightning Champagne Cocktail

Picture this: a boat cruising around Sydney harbour. On the middle deck, a barbecue with hot coals glistening in the night breeze. The music starts 'Oh Lucky You' by the Lightning Seeds and in I walk to prepare this exciting dessert and cocktail as I groove to the sounds in traditional Ainsley style. It tasted great too. Oh lucky you!

Serves 6
225 g (8 oz) large strawberries
3 ripe but firm fresh peaches
2 tablespoons brandy plus extra for flambéeing
2 tablespoons icing sugar
200 g (7 oz) tub of crème fraîche or Greek
   natural yoghurt
maple syrup to serve
For the champagne cocktail:
6 white sugar cubes
1 orange
6 teaspoons brandy
75 cl bottle chilled champagne or dry sparkling
   white wine

Hull the strawberries and halve the peaches, remove the stones and cut them into thick slices. Place them into a large bowl with the 2 tablespoons of brandy and mix together well. Set aside for 30 minutes.

For the champagne cocktails, rub each sugar cube over the surface of the orange so that it picks up the flavour of the zest. Drop each one into a tall-stemmed glass and add 1 teaspoon of the brandy to each. Set aside.

If your barbecue has widely spaced bars, position a fine-meshed rack (see page 16) over the coals and leave it for a couple of minutes to get hot.

Place the pieces of fruit on to the rack and cook for 2 minutes.

Spoon the icing sugar into a fine sieve and dust half of it heavily over the fruits. Turn them over and cook for 2 minutes. Dredge them with the remaining icing sugar, turn over and cook for another 2 minutes until the sugar has lightly caramelized.

Now if you want to, stand back and splash extra teaspoons of brandy over the fruits, taking care because it will ignite as it hits the hot coals. Let the flames die down between each spoonful.

Quickly remove the fruits to individual bowls, spoon over the crème fraîche or yoghurt and drizzle over the maple syrup.

Pour the champagne into the prepared glasses and serve straight away.

Boozy Caramel Oranges with Caramel Brittle Ice Cream

Start to make the ice cream well beforehand to give it plenty of time to freeze. If you wish, you can make it well in advance but you will need to make the caramel in two smaller batches – one for the ice cream, and one for the oranges later. There will be far more ice cream than you will need for this pudding – it will probably make enough to feed 8 people – but it will keep in the freezer for another day (if you're lucky!).

Serves 4

6 small oranges
225 g (8 oz) granulated sugar
150 ml (5 fl oz) water
2 tablespoons orange liqueur such as Cointreau or Grand Marnier

For the ice cream:

600 ml (1 pint) milk
1 vanilla pod, split open lengthways
6 egg yolks
75 g (3 oz) caster sugar
300 ml (10 fl oz) double cream

For the ice cream, bring the milk and the vanilla pod to the boil in a pan (non-stick if possible). Set aside for 20 minutes to allow the flavour of the vanilla to infuse the milk.

Beat the egg yolks and sugar together in a bowl until pale and creamy. Bring the milk back to the boil, discard the vanilla pod and whisk the milk into the egg yolks.

Return the mixture to the pan and cook over a low heat, stirring all the time, until it lightly coats the back of the wooden spoon. Pour the custard into a shallow plastic container and leave to cool. Then transfer to the fridge and leave it to chill for 1 hour.

Stir the cream into the custard and either churn it in an ice cream maker or freeze it until almost firm. Scrape the mixture into a food processor and blitz briefly until smooth. Pour it back into the box and repeat once more.

When the ice cream is almost firm, cut a slice off the top and bottom of each orange and carefully cut away all the skin and white pith. Cut each orange across into about 5 slices, divide them between 4 x 30 cm (12 in) squares of extra-thick foil and bring the edges up around the fruit.

You now need to make some caramel. Put the sugar and the water into a large pan and leave over a low heat until the sugar has completely dissolved. Line a baking tray with some foil and set to one side.

Bring the syrup to the boil and boil vigorously until it has turned a rich caramel colour. Quickly pour half on to the baking tray and leave to set.

Stand back and add the orange liqueur to the caramel left in the pan. It will hiss and splutter alarmingly but don't worry. Return the pan to a low heat and stir until smooth.

Divide the sauce equally between the oranges and scrunch the edges together well to seal. Set aside while you finish the ice cream.

Break the sheet of caramel into little pieces, stir them into the ice cream and return it to the freezer until firm.

Place the orange parcels on to the side of the barbecue and barbecue over medium-hot coals for 8–10 minutes. Lift them on to serving plates, carefully open up each one and serve with a scoop of the ice cream.

Chatachak Fruit Purses with Lemongrass Syrup

I created this dish whilst on my travels in Thailand and wanted to use lots of the natural flavours and fruits of the country. Once tried I think you'll agree it's a 'Chatachak' knockout. (Chatachak is a famous fruit and spice market in Bangkok.)

Serves 4
50 g (2 oz) granulated sugar
65 ml (2½ fl oz) water
1 stick of lemongrass
1 cm (½ in) piece fresh root ginger, peeled
450 g (1 lb) prepared chunks of tropical fruits such as pineapple, mango, papaya, banana and red-skinned apple
1 lime

Put the sugar and water into a pan and bring to a simmer, stirring until the sugar has completely dissolved.
Trim down the lemongrass and then bash it with the back of a large knife to help to release all its flavour.
Cut the piece of ginger into slices and add to the sugar syrup with the lemongrass. Cook for 1–2 minutes.
Remove the pan from the heat and set aside to infuse until the mixture is completely cold. Then remove and discard the pieces of lemongrass and ginger.
Pile about 100 g (4 oz) of fruit into the middle of 4 x 30 cm (12 in) squares of extra-thick foil. Bring the edges of the foil up around the fruit and add about 1½ tablespoons of syrup and a squeeze of lime juice to each one.
Scrunch the edges of the foil together to make well-sealed parcels and cook over medium-hot coals for about 15 minutes.
Lift the parcels on to plates, carefully open them up so that you don't lose any of the juice and eat straight away. These would be good served with a dollop of Denzil's Simple Coconut Ice Cream (see page 162).

Fired Strawberries and Cream

If you're someone who believes that strawberries should only be eaten raw, try these and I'm sure you'll change your mind. They're delicious, especially served with a good dollop of clotted cream. Go on, fire up those tastebuds.

Serves 4
450 g (1 lb) strawberries
4 tablespoons white rum, Cointreau or Kirsch
4 tablespoons light muscovado sugar
2 cinnamon sticks, broken into short pieces
225 g (8 oz) tub of clotted cream or 300 ml (10 fl oz) extra thick double cream to serve

Hull strawberries, cut them in half and place them into a large bowl.
Mix the rum, Cointreau or Kirsch with the sugar until the sugar has dissolved, then stir it into the strawberries.
Shape 4 x 30 cm (12 in) squares of extra-thick foil into little bowls and divide the strawberries and the juice between them. Add a piece of cinnamon stick to each one, bring the edges of the foil together and scrunch the edges together well to seal.
Place the parcels on to the side of the barbecue and cook over medium-hot coals for 4–5 minutes until heated through.
Lift them on to serving plates, open them up and serve with a spoonful of clotted or thick double cream.

OPPOSITE Fired Strawberries and Cream

Honey Nut Baked Fresh Figs

Fresh figs can be a little bland unless you are really lucky to come across a good batch. Cooking them like this improves their flavour and the nuts give everything a nice bit of crunchiness.

Serves 4
12 ripe fresh figs
8 tablespoons clear honey
200 g (7 oz) tub of Greek natural yoghurt
25 g (1 oz) flaked almonds, lightly toasted

Trim the end of the stalk off each fig and then cut a cross into the top of each one and open it up.
Place 3 of the figs into the centre of 4 x 30 cm (12 in) squares of extra-thick foil and bring the edges of the foil up around the sides of the fruit.
Spoon the honey equally over the fruit and then scrunch the edges of the foil together to make well-sealed parcels. Place them to the side of medium-low barbecue and cook for 15 minutes until tender.
Transfer the parcels to plates and open up the foil. Add a good spoonful of Greek yoghurt to each one, sprinkle with the nuts and eat while they're still warm.

Pineapple French Toast Sandwiches

These are lovely served up warm for breakfast and would also make a great dessert, served with some extra thick double cream. The amount of rum that you add to the egg mixture will depend on how much of a kick-start you need first thing in the morning or last thing at night. Substitute the rum with the leftover pineapple juice if you would prefer an alcohol-free sandwich! Ooh la lah.

Serves 4
8 x 1 cm (½ in) thick slices of fresh white bread or brioche
50 g (2 oz) butter, softened
225 g (8 oz) can crushed pineapple
2 teaspoons mixed spice
3 tablespoons demerara sugar
4 large eggs
150 ml (5 fl oz) single cream
1–2 tablespoons dark rum

Spread one side of each slice of bread with a little of the softened butter.
Tip the pineapple into a sieve and press out all the juice into a bowl. Spoon the pineapple into another bowl and stir in ½ teaspoon of mixed spice and 1 tablespoon of the demerara sugar.
Place a large spoonful of the pineapple mixture into the centre of 4 of the buttered bread slices and cover with the remaining slices, butter-side down. Press the edges together well to seal.
Beat the eggs with the cream, rum and another 1 teaspoon of the mixed spice. Pour into a large shallow dish.
Place half the remaining butter in a heavy-based frying pan and leave over a medium-hot barbecue until sizzling.
Dip 2 of the pineapple sandwiches into the egg mixture until well soaked and evenly coated. Add to the pan and cook for about 1 minute on each side until crisp and golden. Remove and repeat with the rest of the butter and the remaining sandwiches.
Lift the sandwiches on to warmed plates and sprinkle with the rest of the demerara sugar mixed with the remaining ½ teaspoon of mixed spice. Cut each one into 2 triangles and eat straight away while still warm.

Mango, Ginger and Orange Kebabs

These would be delicious served for breakfast and could be transformed into a dessert with the addition of a little dark rum to the sauce, served with perhaps some chilled pouring cream.

Serves 4
1 large, ripe but firm mango
3 small oranges
16 small pieces crystallized ginger
3 tablespoons stem ginger syrup
1 tablespoon dark muscovado sugar
1 teaspoon mixed spice
25 g (1 oz) butter, melted

16 x 25 cm (10 in) bamboo skewers soaked in
  cold water for 30 minutes

Peel the mango and then cut the flesh away from either side of the thin, flat stone in 2 thick slices. Cut it into rough 2.5 cm (1 in) chunks.
Take a thin slice off the top and bottom of each orange. Lay them cut-side down on a board, slice away all the skin and white pith and then cut each one across into 6 slices.
Thread 3 pieces of mango, 2 pieces of crystallized ginger and 2 slices of orange alternately on to pairs of parallel bamboo skewers to make 8 kebabs. The slightly spaced-apart skewers will stop everything from spinning around while you cook them.
Put the stem ginger syrup, muscovado sugar, mixed spice and butter into a pan and slowly bring to the boil, stirring. Remove from the heat and leave to cool.
Brush the ginger toffee sauce over the kebabs and barbecue over medium-hot coals for 10 minutes, turning once.

Naughty Danish Pastries

These are actually ready-made croissants stuffed with various 'Danish-like' fillings. Toasting them on the barbecue makes them nice and crisp on the outside and warm and gooey in the centre. Sounds a bit like me?

Serves 6
12 fresh croissants
4 x 15 g (½ oz) rows of plain chocolate squares
50 g (2 oz) marzipan, coarsely grated
4 tablespoons thick apricot conserve or
  mincemeat

Cut a large pocket into the side of each croissant with a small serrated knife.
Put one stick of chocolate, 15 g (½ oz) grated marzipan or 1 tablespoon of either apricot conserve or mincemeat into the centre of each croissant and press them together again.
Just before serving, place the croissants onto the edge of a medium-hot barbecue and cook for just 1 minute on each side until they are lightly toasted and the centres have melted. Serve straight away

Strawberry Hill Pineapple with Rum Butter Glaze

I made this on one of the balconies of the famous 'Strawberry Hill Hotel' overlooking the spectacular Blue Montains of Jamaica. Like the country, this dessert made me feel warm, saucy and sexy. Perhaps it will have the same effect on you?! You will need a clean rack on which to barbecue this dessert so either try to keep a small area clean while you are cooking the meats, or very carefully lift off the rack, leave it to cool and then give it a quick scrub before using.

Serves 4–6
1 large fresh pineapple
caster or icing sugar for sprinkling
75 g (3 oz) unsalted butter
75 g (3 oz) demerara sugar
juice of ½ lime
1 vanilla pod
2 tablespoons dark rum
1 quantity Denzil's Simple Coconut Ice Cream
  (see page 162) to serve

Slice the top and the bottom off the pineapple, sit it upright on a board and cut it in to quarters. Remove the core from each quarter and then slice it across into 2.5 cm (1 in) thick triangular slices.
Sprinkle both sides of each piece of pineapple with a little of the caster or icing sugar and barbecue over medium-hot coals for 5–6 minutes until lightly caramelized.

Meanwhile melt the butter in a small pan and add the demerara sugar and lime juice.
Split the vanilla pod open with the tip of a knife and scrape out the seeds into the pan (the rest of the vanilla pod can be saved for another recipe). Add the rum, set it alight and place it to the side of the barbecue rack. Stir until it has melted and bubbled to form a smooth glaze.
As soon as the pineapple is cooked, remove it from the barbecue on to a plate, spoon over the rum butter glaze and serve at once with a scoop of Denzil's Simple Coconut Ice Cream (page 162).

VARIATION
You can also make this dessert using bananas. Barbecue the unpeeled bananas over medium-hot coals for about 10–15 minutes (depending on how ripe they are), turning them carefully every now and then, until they are virtually black all over and tender. Lift them on to a plate and make a slit in the skin of each one. Pull back the skin slightly, spoon in some of the rum butter glaze and serve straight away, sprinkled with a little ground cinnamon if you wish.

OPPOSITE Strawberry Hill Pineapple with Rum Butter Glaze and Denzil's Simple Coconut Ice Cream (see page 162)

DO-AHEAD DESSERTS

Red Summer Berries in Sparkling White Wine

This must be one of the easiest puddings in the world! Just have the berry mixture all ready in the glasses and simply top up with some sparkling white wine when you are ready to serve. If you're feeling posh, why not use champagne... lots of it!

Serves 6
100 g (4 oz) small strawberries
100 g (4 oz) raspberries
100 g (4 oz) blackberries
100 g (4 oz) blueberries
finely grated zest of 1 small orange
3 tablespoons brandy
4 tablespoons caster sugar
75 cl bottle of chilled sparkling dry white wine

Hull the strawberries, cut them in half and place them in a bowl with the raspberries, blackberries and blueberries. Stir in the orange zest, brandy and caster sugar.
Spoon the mixture into 6 tall wine glasses, cover and chill for 1 hour.
When you are ready, pour over just enough sparkling wine to cover the fruits and serve straight away while they're still fizzing.

Denzil's Simple Coconut Ice Cream

This is very rich and utterly delicious. You could serve it with some prepared fresh tropical fruits, strawberries or simply scoop over the pulp of some fresh passionfruit.

Serves 6
400 ml (14 fl oz) canned coconut milk
4 medium egg yolks
75 g (3 oz) caster sugar
200 ml (7 fl oz) double cream

Put the coconut milk into a non-stick pan and slowly bring to the boil.
Meanwhile, whisk the egg yolks and sugar together in a bowl until pale and creamy.
Whisk the hot coconut milk into the egg yolks, return the mixture to the pan and cook over a gentle heat, stirring, until it lightly coats the back of the wooden spoon.
Pour the mixture into a shallow plastic container, stir in the double cream and leave until cool. Then cover and chill in the fridge for 1 hour.
Now you can either churn the mixture in an ice cream maker or slide the container into the freezer and leave it until almost firm.
Scrape the mixture into a food processor and blitz briefly until smooth. Pour back into the box and repeat once more.
Return the ice cream to the freezer and leave until very firm or until required. If the ice cream has been made some time in advance, remove it from the freezer to the fridge about 30 minutes before serving to allow it time to soften slightly.

Yum Yum Blackcurrant and Cream Jellies

You can also make these refreshing little jellies with redcurrants if you wish. My kids love them. Unfortunately, so do all the other kids down my street.

Serves 4
450 ml (15 fl oz) cold water plus 3 tablespoons
2 tablespoons powdered gelatine
225 g (8 oz) blackcurrants, stalks removed
100 g (4 oz) granulated sugar
1–2 tablespoons crème de cassis (optional)
For the cream jelly:
45 g (1½ oz) caster sugar
pared zest of ½ lemon
300 ml (10 fl oz) milk
150 ml (5 fl oz) single cream
1½ tablespoons cold water
1 tablespoon powdered gelatine
whipped cream, 4 strings fresh blackcurrants and
  mint sprigs to decorate

Put the 3 tablespoons of cold water into a small pan. Sprinkle over the gelatine and set aside for 5 minutes.

Meanwhile, put the blackcurrants, sugar and the rest of the water into a pan and bring to the boil. Leave to simmer for about 4 minutes until the fruit has softened and then press the mixture through a sieve into a bowl to remove all the little seeds.

Heat the pan of gelatine over a low heat until clear. Stir it into the blackcurrant mixture and pour into 4 wine glasses, tumblers or small bowls. Chill in the fridge for about 4 hours until set.

For the cream jelly, put the sugar, strips of lemon zest, milk and cream into a pan and leave over a low heat until the sugar has dissolved. Set aside until cold.

Place the 1½ tablespoons of cold water into a small pan and sprinkle over the second amount of gelatine. Leave for 5 minutes and then heat gently until clear. Strain the milky mixture into a bowl and stir in the gelatine.

By now the blackcurrant jellies should be set. Pour a layer of the cream jelly on top of each one and chill for another 2 hours or until set.

Just before serving, decorate each jelly with a dollop of whipped cream, a string of blackcurrants and a sprig of fresh mint if you wish.

Iced Fresh Fruit Platter with Passionfruit Cream

I like to leave the skin on the fruits for this dessert, so that you've got something to hang on to when you dip it into the cream. To serve less people, just cut down on the number of different fruits that you use, but do keep their colour in mind when making your selection. Remember, there's nothing like a bit of colour... so my wife keeps telling me.

Serves 8
3 ripe peaches or nectarines
3 red-skinned apples
1 large bunch of red or green grapes
8 ripe fresh figs
1 small Galia or Charentais melon or a large
  wedge of watermelon
8 ripe apricots
For the passionfruit cream:
4 passionfruit
150 ml (5 fl oz) double cream
finely grated zest of ½ small orange
2 tablespoons icing sugar or more to taste
2 tablespoons orange juice
5 tablespoons Greek natural yoghurt
plenty of crushed ice to serve

For the passionfruit cream, cut the passionfruit in half and scoop out the pulp into a bowl.
Whip the cream, orange zest and the icing sugar into soft peaks and then gradually whisk in the orange juice, yoghurt and passionfruit pulp so that the mixture remains softly whipped. Spoon the mixture into a small serving bowl, cover and set aside to chill in the fridge.

Cut the fruits into one-portion pieces. Place on a tray, cover with clingfilm and chill in the fridge until just before you are ready to serve.
Cover a large, round serving plate or tray with lots of crushed ice and nestle the bowl of passionfruit cream in the centre. Arrange the chilled prepared fruits attractively over the ice and serve straight away.

VARIATION

You can vary the selection of fruits, depending on availability or according to a theme if you wish. Red fruits such as strawberries, cherries, plums, red-skinned apples and red grapes would work well with 300 g (10 oz) of Greek yoghurt mixed with 2 tablespoons of lemon curd and the finely grated zest and juice of 1 small lemon. For an Italian theme serve fresh figs, peaches, pears, green grapes and melon, with perhaps a bowl of slightly sweetened mascarpone cheese. For a tropical theme use papaya, mangoes, pineapple, kiwi fruit, melon and serve with the passionfruit cream.

ABOVE Ooh, what a lovely bunch! St Mary's banana plantation, Jamaica.
OPPOSITE Iced Fresh Fruit Platter with Passionfruit Cream

Nicos' and Athanasia's Apricot Yoghurt Brûlée

Before the days of grills, brûlées were made by heating metal discs in the fire until red hot and then holding them over a sugar-coated surface until it turned to caramel. You can now buy nifty little sets which imitate this method, and they are great fun to use at a barbecue because the plates can be heated on the rack over the coals and then used to caramelize already prepared puddings just before you need them. However, here is a recipe using an ordinary grill for those of you like me without one of these sets.

Serves 6
600 g (1¼ lb) apricot compote or fresh apricots
finely grated zest of 1 lemon (optional)
750 g (1½ lb) Greek natural yoghurt
175 g (6 oz) light soft brown sugar

Cut the apricots in half and remove the stones. Slice them into 6 small terracota dishes that are 10 cm (4 in) in diameter and 2.5 cm (1 in) deep so that they cover the bases in a thick layer.
Stir the lemon zest, if using, into the yoghurt and then spoon it in a thick even layer over the apricots. If the yoghurt was not icy cold, leave the dish in the fridge for at least 1 hour until it is really well chilled. This will prevent it from curdling when you caramelize the top of the pudding.
Preheat the grill on its hottest setting.
Sprinkle the sugar over the top of the yoghurt in a thick even layer, making sure that it touches the sides of the dish so that none of the yoghurt is peeping through, then wipe the edges clean.
Place the dish on to the grill pan and slide it under a very hot grill for about 3 minutes, turning the dish now and then if necessary so that all the sugar caramelizes evenly.
Remove the dish from under the grill and leave it for a few minutes until the sugar has cooled and gone hard before serving. But don't leave it any more than 10 minutes or the caramel will turn into syrup!

Mean Mango and Lime Sorbet

The amount of lime that you need for this sorbet will depend on the ripeness of the mangoes and how juicy the limes are. You want the mixture to be a little sharp as well as sweet before you freeze it. 'Don't be mean with the mango.'

Serves 6–8
2–3 limes
75 g (3 oz) granulated sugar
75 ml (3 fl oz) water
3 large mangoes
lime wedges and sprigs of fresh mint to decorate

Thinly pare the zest from the limes and then squeeze out the juice. Put the sugar, water and lime zest into a small pan and leave over a low heat until the sugar has completely dissolved.
Now bring the mixture to the boil, lower the heat and leave to simmer for 5 minutes. Set aside and leave to go cold and then chill in the fridge for a few hours until it's icy cold.
Peel the mangoes and slice the flesh away from the stone into a food processor. Strain over the lime syrup, add the lime juice and give everything a quick whizz until very smooth.
Now you can ether churn the mixture in an ice cream maker or pour it into a shallow plastic container (it will freeze quicker this way), cover and freeze until almost firm.
Scrape the mixture back into the food processor and give it another whizz until very smooth. Scrape it back into the box, return to the freezer and repeat the process once more. Then leave it to freeze for about 3 hours until firm.
Serve scoops of the sorbet in chilled dessert glasses, decorated with the lime wedges and sprigs of fresh mint.

Blue Mountain Coffee Granita

The finished texture of this very light and refreshing dessert should be like large flakes of sea salt. Once in your mouth, close your eyes and capture the taste of the Caribbean.

Serves 6–8
600 ml (1 pint) water
100 g (4 oz) granulated sugar
50 g (2 oz) Blue Mountain coffee beans or ready-ground Continental Roast coffee
150 ml (5 fl oz) double cream
1 teaspoon drinking chocolate powder
12–16 coffee beans to decorate

Put the water and sugar into a pan and leave over a low heat until the sugar has dissolved.
If you are using whole coffee beans, grind them to a powder in a coffee grinder. Stir the ground coffee into the sugar syrup and leave to infuse for 5 minutes.
Strain the coffee through a filter paper or a fine sieve lined with a piece of muslin into a shallow plastic container. Leave until cool and then cover and put into the freezer until the mixture begins to freeze around the edges.
Scrape all the frozen ice away from the sides and break it up into smaller crystals with a fork. Return it to the freezer and continue to do this, every 30 minutes or so, until you have a frozen but still grainy mixture.
To serve, whip the cream into soft peaks. Spoon the granita into glasses, top with a spoonful of cream and decorate with a sprinkling of drinking chocolate powder and a couple of coffee beans.

OPPOSITE Blue Mountain Coffee Granita

NON-ALCOHOLIC DRINKS

Iced Melon Limeade

The colour of your finished drink will depend entirely on the type of melon that you use. Watermelon will give you a pink drink, Charentais melon will make it orange and Galia or Ogen melon will turn it green.

Makes 1 x 1.75 litre (3 pint) jug, enough for about 8 glasses
13 limes
450 g (1 lb) peeled and seeded melon flesh such as watermelon, Charentais or Galia melon
100 g (4 oz) caster sugar
2 trays of ice cubes (about 750 g (1½ lb), crushed
chilled sparkling mineral water

Cut 1 lime in half and slice very thinly. Set aside. Finely grate the zest of another 2 limes and then squeeze out the juice of all 12.
Put the lime zest, lime juice, melon flesh and sugar into a liquidizer or food processor and blend until smooth.
Put the crushed ice cubes into a chilled 1.75 litre (3 pint) glass jug, pour in the limeade and top up with sparkling water. Add the lime slices, give everything a quick stir and serve.

TIPPLE TIP: Add a dash of Midori, a lime flavoured liqueur, to each glass

Mango and Pineapple Cooler

This drink is flavoured with fresh ginger and then topped up with sparkling ginger beer.

Makes 1 x 1.75 litre (3 pint) jug, enough for about 8 glasses
75 g (3 oz) caster sugar
150 ml (5 fl oz) water
8 slices fresh root ginger
1 small, very ripe fresh pineapple or 550 g (1¼ lb) prepared pineapple
1 ripe mango
juice of 2 small lemons
plenty of ice cubes
450 ml (15 fl oz) sparkling ginger beer

Heat the sugar and water in a pan until clear. Add the sliced ginger, bring to the boil and leave to simmer for 2 minutes. Leave to cool and then chill in the fridge for 2 hours.
If you are using a fresh pineapple, slice off the top and the bottom and cut away all the skin and the little brown 'eyes'. Cut it into quarters, remove the core and roughly chop the flesh. Simply discard the core from the prepared pineapple and then chop. Peel the mango and slice the flesh away from the stone.
Put the pineapple and mango into a liquidizer or food processor and strain over the chilled ginger syrup. Blend until very smooth.
Fill a chilled 1.75 litre (3 pint) glass jug with ice and pour over the pineapple mixture and the lemon juice. Top up with the ginger beer, give everything a good stir and serve.

TIPPLE TIP: Add a dash of white rum to each glass

Tangy Lemon Fizz

This is probably the best version of lemonade in the world!

Makes 1 x 1.75 litre (3 pint) jug, enough for about 8 glasses
8 lemons
225 g (8 oz) caster sugar
plenty of ice cubes
900 ml (1½ pints) sparkling mineral water

Remove the zest from 4 of the lemons in long thin strips with a cannelling knife and set aside. Coarsely grate the zest off the rest of the lemons.
Squeeze the juice from all the lemons and mix it with the lemon zest and sugar until the sugar has completely dissolved.
Fill a chilled 1.75 litre (3 pint) glass jug with ice, twisting the long strips of zest in amongst them. Add the lemon mixture, top up with the sparkling mineral water and give everything a good stir before serving.

 TIPPLE TIP: Add a dash of gin to each glass

Elderflower and Strawberry 'Champagne'

This drink seems to resemble a perfect English summer's day. Fingers crossed!

Makes 1 x 1.75 litre (3 pint) jug, enough for about 8 glasses
225 g (8 oz) small strawberries, hulled
2 lemons, halved and thinly sliced
150 ml (5 fl oz) elderflower cordial
900 ml (1½ pints) sparkling apple juice such as Appletize

Halve the strawberries and place one half into each compartment of 2 ice cube trays. Top up with water and freeze until hard.
Mix the strawberry ice cubes and lemon slices together in a 1.75 litre (3 pint) glass jug.
Add the elderflower cordial and the sparkling apple juice and give everything a good stir before serving.

 TIPPLE TIP: Add a dash of Cointreau to each glass

Iced Apple and Mint Tea

The apple and mint ice cubes are not essential but they do add a nice fruity tang to the finished drink.

Makes 1 x 1.75 litre (3 pint) jug, enough for about 8 glasses
450 g (1 lb) cooking apples, peeled, cored and sliced
150 ml (5 fl oz) water
300 ml (10 fl oz) apple juice or water
25 g (1 oz) fresh mint sprigs
6 apple-flavoured tea bags
1.2 litres (2 pints) boiling water
5 tablespoons caster sugar or to taste
2 Granny Smith apples, sliced

Put the cooking apples into a pan with the water. Cover and cook for 5 minutes or until soft. Set aside to go cold.
Spoon the purée into a food processor and add the apple juice or water and the leaves from 4–5 sprigs of the mint. Blend until smooth. Pour the mixture into 2 ice cubes trays and freeze until hard.
Place the tea bags and another 6 large sprigs of the mint into a heatproof jug. Pour on the boiling water and leave for 5 minutes.
Lift out the tea bags and the mint and stir in the sugar. Leave until cool, then chill in the fridge until icy cold.
Tip the apple and mint ice cubes into a 1.75 litre (3 pint) glass jug and add the remaining mint sprigs and the sliced apples. Pour in the cold tea, give everything a good stir and serve straight away in tall glasses.

 TIPPLE TIP: Add a dash of dark rum or bourbon to each glass

ALCOHOLIC DRINKS

Margarita Fizz

This is just like the classic Mexican cocktail, but diluted down with sparkling water so that each drink is less potent and (hopefully) lasts a lot longer.

Makes 2 x 1.2 litre (2 pint) jugs, enough for about 14 glasses
14 limes
100 g (4 oz) caster sugar plus 1 tablespoon
600 ml (1 pint) tequila
250 ml (8 fl oz) orange liqueur such as Orange
    Curaçao, Triple Sec or Cointreau
plenty of crushed ice
a few whole ice cubes (about 2 trays)
1.2 litres (2 pints) sparkling mineral water

Place the glasses in the freezer with two 1.2 litre (2 pint) glass jugs for a few hours to frost.
Meanwhile, thinly slice 2 of the limes and set aside. Finely pare the zest off half the remaining limes with a potato peeler, taking care not to remove any of the bitter white pith underneath.
Squeeze out the juice from all the limes and stir in all but 1 tablespoon of the sugar until dissolved. Stir in the tequila and the orange liqueur.
Just before serving, spread 1 tablespoon of sugar on to a plate. Remove the glasses from the freezer, rub the rims with half a lime and press them into the sugar. Pack each one with some crushed ice. Make a cut into the centre of each lime slice and slide over the edge of each glass.
Remove the jugs from the freezer and add a few whole ice cubes and some lime zest to each one. Pour half the lime and tequila mixture and half the sparkling water into each jug, give everything a good stir and serve in the prepared glasses.

Sangria Sparkle

This is very refreshing summertime drink. You can make up the fruit and wine base in advance and simply add the ice cubes and fizzy water just before serving.

Makes 2 x 1 litre (1¾ pint) jugs, enough for about 12 glasses
3 small oranges, sliced
3 lemons, sliced
plenty of ice
600 ml (1 pint) freshly squeezed orange juice
juice of 2 lemons
75 g (3 oz) caster sugar
75 cl bottle of light, fruity red wine such as a
    Chianti or Beaujolais
150 ml (5 fl oz) brandy
600 ml (1 pint) sparkling mineral water

Fill two 1 litre (1¾ pint) glass jugs with the sliced fruits and the ice.
Mix together the orange and lemon juices with the sugar until the sugar has dissolved. Stir in the wine, brandy and water. Pour the mixture into the prepared jugs and serve straight away.

OPPOSITE, CLOCKWISE FROM TOP Elderflower and Strawberry 'Champagne' (see page 171), Iced Melon Lemonade (see page 170), Sangria Sparkle and Ainsley's Mum's Caribbean Rum Pu-Punch (see page 174)
BELOW Delicious grapes from the Cape. South Africa.

Ainsley's Mum's Caribbean Rum Pu-Punch

I have watched my Mum make this a thousand times. If you can't find canned mango pulp, just whizz a 400 g (14 oz) can of mango pieces in the liquidizer until smooth. You can leave out the rum for a non-alcoholic punch if you wish.

Makes 2 x 1.75 litre (3 pint) jugs, enough for about 16 glasses

175 g (6 oz) granulated sugar
175 ml (6 fl oz) boiling water
juice of 4 limes and 4 lemons
1 teaspoon angostura bitters
400 ml (14 fl oz) canned mango pulp
150 ml (5 fl oz) strawberry syrup (optional)
250–300 ml (8–10 fl oz) white rum (remember, more rum, more dancing)
1 litre (1¾ pints) tropical fruit juice
1 litre (1¾ pints) lemonade or sparkling mineral water
plenty of ice
quartered lime and orange slices to decorate

Stir the sugar and water together until the sugar has dissolved. Leave to go cold.
Mix the sugar syrup with the lime juice, lemon juice, angostura bitters, mango pulp, strawberry syrup, if using, and rum and stir together until well mixed. This can now be set aside and chilled until just before you are ready to serve.
Stir in the fruit juice and lemonade and serve over ice cubes, decorated with lime and orange slices.

South African White Wine and Peach Cup

You could use a dry South African Chardonnay or Sauvignon Blanc for this drink.

Makes 1 x 1.75 litre (3 pint) jug, enough for about 8–10 glasses
300 ml (10 fl oz) peach schnapps
2 tablespoons caster sugar
juice of 2 large lemons
2–3 ripe peaches
plenty of ice cubes
75 cl bottle chilled dry white wine
450 ml (15 fl oz) chilled sparkling mineral water

Put the peach schnapps, sugar and lemon juice into a jug and stir until the sugar has dissolved.
Cut each peach in half, remove the stones and thinly slice the flesh.
Fill a 1.75 litre (3 pint) glass jug with ice cubes and pour in the peach schnapps mixture, wine and sparkling mineral water. Add the sliced peaches, give everything a good stir and serve straight away in large wine glasses.

Shake-e-Up Coffee Cocktail

This deliciously creamy cocktail made with muscovado sugar and coffee beans from the famous Blue Mountains of Jamaica really packs a punch! You can simply replace the fresh coffee and water mixture and the sugar with 2 tablespoons of Camp Coffee essence if you prefer.

Serves 8–10
50 g (2 oz) coffee beans, finely ground
120 ml (4 fl oz) boiling water
6 tablespoons light muscovado sugar
120 ml (4 fl oz) Tia Maria or Kahlua
120 ml (4 fl oz) dark rum
250 ml (8 fl oz) double cream
½ teaspoon vanilla essence
plenty of crushed ice
freshly grated nutmeg for dusting

Put the ground coffee beans into a jug or a cafetière if you have one. Pour on the boiling water and leave for 5 minutes. Strain off, through a coffee filter or muslin-lined sieve if necessary, stir in the muscovado sugar and leave to go cold.
When you are ready, put the cold coffee, Tia Maria, rum, double cream and vanilla essence into a cocktail shaker and shake vigorously.
Fill some glasses with plenty of crushed ice, pour over the coffee cocktail and lightly dust the tops with a little nutmeg before serving.

THEMED BARBECUE MENUS

Here are a few suggestions of dishes you could include if you wish to give a themed barbecue. The amount that you need to cook will depend on the number of people you wish to feed.

THAILAND

Orla's Bamboo Thai Prawn Satay with Griddled Limes (page 47)

Million Meaty Satay Sticks (page 43) with Speckled Spicy Peanut Sauce (page 30)

—

Hua Hin Beach Red Snapper (page 108)

Balinese Chicken (page 58)

Korma Courgette and Chickpea Burgers (page 111)

—

Nice Rice Noodle Doodle Salad (page 138)

Cool Carrot, Cumin and Lemon Salad (page 144)

—

Chatachak Fruit Purses in Lemon Grass Syrup (page 156)

Mean Mango and Lime Sorbet (page 167) with
Denzil's Simple Coconut Ice Cream (page 162)

—

Iced Melon Limeade (page 170)

Chilled Tiger Beer

Topping up the tan and not a
factor 15 in sight!
Near Mount Connor, Australia.

A CLASSIC BRITISH BARBECUE

Buffalo Chicken Wings with Blue Cheese Dip (page 44)

Fire-roasted Red Pepper Guacamole (page 42)

—

Classic Brilliant Beefburgers (page 88)

Cumberland Sausage Catherine Wheel (page 92)

Maple Glazed Pork Spare Ribs (page 67)

Korma Courgette and Chickpea Burgers (page 111)

—

Salt 'n' Pepper Fire-baked Tatties (page 127)

—

Minted Cucumber and Cherry Tom Tom Salad (page 146)

New Potato Salad with Gherkins, Chives and Soured Cream (page 142)

The Best Barbecue Garlic Butter Bread (page 148)

—

Fired Strawberries and Cream (page 156)

Yum Yum Blackcurrant and Cream Jellies (page 163)

—

Plenty of Chilled Sparkling White Wine

A Barrel of Ale

Elderflower and Strawberry Champagne (page 171)

GREECE

Melintzanosalata with Cherry Tomato Sticks (page 48)

Garlic Pitta Fingers (page 150)

Mamma Tahsia's Baked Greek Olives (page 46)

—

St Giorgio's Kleftiko Parcels (page 70)

Beef Peppa-feta Rolls (page 83)

Chargrilled Squid Stuffed with Spinach and Mint (page 95)

Whole Grilled Aubergines
with Tricolour Stuffing (page 123)

—

Tangier Mint Tabbouleh (page 138)

Creamy Crisp Green Salad
(with the Creamy Garlic Dressing) (page 142)

—

Honey Nut Baked Figs (page 158)

Nicos' and Athanasia's Apricot Yoghurt Brûlée (page 166)

—

Sangria Sparkle (page 172)

Tangy Lemon Fizz (page 171)

JAMAICA

Spicy Mean Bean Dip with Plantain Chips (page 50)

Dream Stuffed Mild Anaheim Chillies (page 46)

—

Fuzzyless Jerk Chicken (page 55)

Sweet Chilli King Prawns (page 104)

Jammin' Baked Pumpkin with Vegetable and Coconut Curry (page 122)

—

Husky Jacket Corn On The Cob with Chilli and Spring Onion Dressing (page 128)

Peppy's Jamaican Rice and Peas (page 144)

Ainsley's Ultimate Creole Cabbage Salad (page 139)

—

Strawberry Hill Pineapple (page 160) with Rum Butter Glaze with Denzil's
Simple Coconut Ice Cream (page 162)

Blue Mountain Coffee Granita (page 168)

—

Ainsley's Mum's Caribbean Rum Pu-Punch (page 174)

Mango and Pineapple Cooler (page 170)

AUSTRALIA

Yakitori Skewers (page 51)

Fire-roasted Red Pepper Guacamole (page 42)

—

Barbecued Lobster with Three Flavoured Butters (page 94)

Alan and Andy's Aussie Steaks (page 79) with Shallot, Mustard
and Black Peppercorn Butter (page 31)

Marinated Halloumi Cheese with Tang! Tang! Dressing (page 116)

Fire-roasted Mediterranean Vegetables (page 110)

—

Creamy Crisp Green Salad with Guacamole Dressing (page 142)

Cor! Puy Lentil, Red Onion and Sundried Tomato Salad (page 140)

—

Sydney Flambéed Fruits with Maple Syrup and Lightning Cocktail (page 154)

Red Summer Berries in Sparkling Wine (page 162)

—

Iced Apple and Mint Tea (page 171)

Sangria Sparkle (page 172)

Wilna's Fruit Farm 'Behind'.
Butterflied leg of lamb 'Upfront'.

SOUTH AFRICA

Buffalo Chicken Wings with Blue Cheese Dip (page 44)

Parker's Pear and Parma Ham Brushcetta (page 42)

—

Butterflied Studded Leg of Lamb (page 76)

Jim's Barbecued Tuna and Chips (page 99)

Spinach and Blue Cheese Mushroom Cups (page 118)

—

Cumin-crusted Butternut Squash (page 131)

Fire-roasted Red Pepper and Nectarine Salad (page 143)

—

Boozy Caramel Oranges with Caramel Brittle Ice Cream (page 155)

Iced Fresh Fruit Platter with Passionfruit Cream (page 164)

—

South African White Wine and Peach Cup (page 175)

Tangy Lemon Fizz (page 171)

BARBECUE SUPPLIERS

It is not always easy to know where to go to buy a barbecue or to find the specific barbecue that you are looking for. Try the following retailers:

- DIY stores, department stores and garden centres all stock barbecues and accessories, especially during the summer months.
- Supermarkets, especially the larger superstores, stock a suprisingly wide range or barbecues, fuels and accessories today.
- Petrol stations stock disposable barbecues, charcoal and firelighters etc. during the summer months.
- Hardware stores and camping shops will stock the gas cylinders for a gas barbecue and probably charcoal too.
- The Barbeque Shop at 46A Portsmouth Road, Cobham, Kent, (01932) 866 044, stocks a wide selection of charcoal and gas barbecues and operates a mail order service.
- Lakeland Plastics, (01539) 488 100, supply portable barbecues and accessories by mail order.
- Special cookware shops usually carry a range of cooking accessories.
- British Gas Energy Centres supply gas barbecues. Ring 0800 850 900 for details of your nearest store.

And here are a few numbers of barbecue manufacturers who will be able to give you the name and address of your local stockists:

Weber charcoal and gas barbecues (01462) 475 000
Outdoor Chef gas barbecues (01784) 421 006
Landmann charcoal and gas barbecues (01299) 251 747 /250 909
Barbecook charcoal and gas barbecues
Black Knight barbecues (01622) 671 771
Odell charcoal and gas barbecues (01352) 762 061
Camping Gaz gas barbecues (0800) 317 466

Still jammin', still smiling. Life is so sweet!

GO ON, GET SIZZLING!!

ACKNOWLEDGEMENTS

A special thanks to Debbie Major for all her hard work. What a star.

To my home economists on location: Orla Broderick and Merrilees Parker. Their input and on-the-spot barbie creations were exemplary. To all the crew: Ben Warwick, Roulla Xenides, Jane Lomas, Andy Morton, Alan Duxbury, Nigel Davey, Lisa Kendrick, Sue Ashcroft and all the Barbecue Bible staff. To everyone at BBC Books for all their support and to my agent and friend, Jeremy Hicks. To my darling wife Clare and children Jimmy and Madeleine for giving me the time and space in which to complete this book.

Thanks also to Julia Schurer on behalf of Weber for all her help and provision of the barbecues for testing, photography and filming; Christine Stokes and Kevan Roe at Chartan-Aldred for all their help and advice and providing us with the charcoal for the recipe testing; Jeff Hull at Landmann, Mervyn at Parlour Products and Pip Smitham of the Barbeque Shop for all their helpful advice, information and provision of all the barbecue accessories; David Beasley, Maggie Mayhew, Sara Buenfeld and Louise Tyler for their help with the recipe testing; Julie Beresford for assisting on the food photography sessions; Matthew Drennan for providing us with a garden in which to test recipes.